Beautiful Feet

A Study in the Book of Romans

Written by Margy Hill with Leroy Hill

Beautiful Feet

Bringing a Message of Peace to a World in Pieces

Introduction

How then shall they call on Him in whom they have not believed? And how shall they believe in Him of whom they have not heard? And how shall they hear without a preacher? And how shall they preach unless they are sent? As it is written: "How beautiful are the feet of those who preach the gospel of peace, who bring glad tidings of good things (Romans 10:14-16)!"

What does it mean to have beautiful feet? Romans 10:15 is not concerned with the external beauty of our feet, but the beauty of the message that we bear. Those with beautiful feet are those who preach the gospel of peace and bring the good news of Jesus Christ! The Greek word *hōraios,* translated *beautiful*, can also be rendered *timely*, which means belonging to the right hour or season. This word conveys the sense of arriving at just the right time. In other words, "How timely are the feet (that is the arrival of) those proclaiming the good news!" Your feet are beautiful because they are designed to bring a timely message of peace to a world that is in pieces.

To be *in pieces* means to be shattered or broken. Everything in the world is broken. Our government is broken, our financial system is broken, and our schools are broken. Let's bring that reality a little closer to home. Our cities are broken, our neighborhoods are broken, and our families are broken. This means, that in the very things these institutions were designed to bring: peace, safety, and comfort, they are powerless to accomplish. Now is the time to preach the gospel of peace, to bring the good news of Jesus Christ! Christ alone has the power to transform and restore that which is broken.

Now that we know that God wants to use our beautiful feet, the question becomes are they willing to go? Doubt, fear, and insecurities keep our feet from walking into the darkness to bring the light of the gospel message. This study is designed to help you overcome your fears and challenge you to use your beautiful feet to bring the good news to those God has placed in your sphere of influence. Part of the armor of God, as described by the apostle Paul, is the shoes of "the preparation of the gospel of peace." The sandals of the Roman soldier "often were fitted with nails, or armed with spikes, to make them hold firm in the ground."[i] God's good news, and our marching orders to preach it, serve as our firm foundation. When we truly allow ourselves to take comfort in the good news promised by God, no forces that the world can marshal will trouble our hearts or give us reason to be afraid. Christ has overcome the world (John 16:33), and we have nothing to fear from it!

Therefore, the purpose of our time in the Book of Romans will be twofold: First, we want to gain a deeper understanding of the gospel and its power to save. Second, we want to learn how to live out the truths of the gospel, in order to daily bear witness to the transforming power of Christ. With these two goals deeply rooted in our minds and hearts, our beautiful feet will be ready and willing to proclaim salvation to everyone.

Lessons

Beautiful Feet

How to Study

Welcome to *Beautiful Feet*, a study through the Book of Romans. Here are some suggestions to help you enjoy a daily, rich, satisfying time with God in His Word. Before you begin each day, open your Bible and pray over the passage you will be reading. Allow your mind and heart to be opened to the teaching of the Holy Spirit.

Lesson Commentary

Begin each week of your study by carefully reading the assigned text and the lesson commentary. This exercise is designed to provide you with focus and direction for the week. As you read your commentary, highlight or circle main points and key areas of interest regarding the passage.

Memory Verse

Each week a verse has been selected from the passage you are studying to memorize and hide in your heart. Scripture memorization is one of the many valuable Christian disciplines believers enjoy.

Daily Lessons

This study has been designed with 5 daily lessons to help you develop a structured quiet time. Plan to study a minimum of 45 minutes each day in order to pray over your lesson, answer questions, and digest what you have learned. Students who study on a daily basis will profit immensely from their discipline.

Reflection

Day 5 of your study is a day of *reflection*. It is an opportunity to ponder what you have learned throughout the week in order to gain personal application. Spending time in prayer and meditating on what you have learned, will allow the Holy Spirit to speak to the areas of your life He desires to impact. Take this time to note how you will act upon what God has revealed to you during the week.

Glossary

A glossary, including 20 key terms from the Book of Romans is available to help you answer several of the questions in the study. These definitions are not exhaustive. They were selected to help provide a basic understanding of the theological themes covered throughout the book.

LESSON I: THE GOSPEL
The Power of God for Salvation
Romans 1:1-17

LESSON I
Romans 1:1-17

THE GOSPEL
The Power of God for Salvation

LESSON 1 COMMENTARY

In the book of Romans, the gospel is exalted. Paul was God's chosen messenger, designated and set apart by God to preach the gospel. His heart was to take the gospel to Rome, because it was the capital of the leading world power. In fact, a popular aphorism stated, "All roads lead to Rome." Why was this a popular saying? Because Rome paved roads throughout its expansive empire. Paved roads made travel to and from Rome a safe and easy affair. The roads were safe because they were constantly patrolled and paved roads made travel easy. Paved roads also expanded Rome's influence because it made the movement of its military and its economy more efficient. Yet, there was a hidden and more meaningful benefit that came with paved roads: *information traveled faster.*

When the roads were paved, God sent forth the gospel to remove the yoke of bondage from sin and to receive children to Himself. Galatians 4:4 states, "But when the fullness of the time had come, God sent forth His Son," to which the writers of the Bible Knowledge Commentary state, "This *time* was when the Roman civilization had brought peace and a road system which facilitated travel; when the Grecian civilization provided a language which was adopted as the lingua franca (adopted common language) of the empire; when the Jews had proclaimed monotheism and the messianic hope in the synagogues of the Mediterranean world."[ii] "The fullness of time," includes the idea that the timing was God's choosing. At the right time in history, His chosen messenger, the apostle Paul, would carry the message of the gospel throughout the world.

The gospel is the good news that breathes life into the spiritually dead hearts of mankind. The famed theologian, Martin Luther anguished over the depths of his own depravity. His agonizing struggle with sin left him frustrated and fearful, wondering how could he ever escape damnation. The Holman New Testament Commentary states, "When the first rays of the gospel began to dawn in Martin Luther's heart, he knew he had the answer. To be righteous, he discovered, one must live by faith—*sola fide*—by faith alone. Luther's discovery of the gospel transformed a moribund monk into a channel of power that infused life into a near-dead church"[iii]

Friends, we are embarking on the journey of a lifetime. A study through the book of Romans! Our hope for you is two-fold. If you are struggling, we hope that your faith, like Luther's, will be quickened and made anew. And, if you are not currently sharing the gospel, we hope that you will receive strength, boldness, and a passion to do so. Enjoy the journey!

MEMORY VERSE

"For I am not ashamed of the gospel of Christ, for it is the power of God to salvation for everyone who believes, for the Jew first and also for the Greek (Romans 1:16)."

Day 1
Gospel Glimpses

"Romans is really the chief part of the New Testament and the very purest Gospel, and is worthy not only that every Christian should know it word for word, by heart, but occupy himself with it every day, as the daily bread of the soul. It can never be read or pondered too much, and the more it is dealt with the more precious it becomes, and the better it tastes – Martin Luther."[iv]

Read Romans 1:1:7.

In Paul's opening greeting to the church in Rome, we see how the gospel, the good news of Jesus Christ, is to function as the centerpiece for the believer's devotional life and evangelistic mission. The gospel is the good news that Christ lived a perfect life, died on the cross, and rose from the dead to satisfy God's wrathful judgment on the world. Because of Jesus' payment in full for our debt, it is now possible for anyone to receive salvation through a living faith in Christ.

1. In Romans 1:1, Paul identifies himself as a bondservant of Jesus Christ, who was called to be an apostle and separated to the gospel of God. Paul knew who he belonged to and who he served. Look up the following verses and describe what it means to *purchased*, *called* and *set apart* as a believer in Jesus Christ.

   • 1 Corinthians 6:20

   • 2 Corinthians 6:17

   • 1 Peter 2:9

2. C. I. Scofield summarizes this idea of being set apart by God writing that "separation is whatever is contrary to the mind of God and unto God Himself. The underlying principle is that in a moral universe it is impossible for God fully to bless and use His children who are in compromise or complicity with evil. Separation from evil implies separation in desire, motive, and act, from the world...Separation is not from contact with evil... but from complicity with and conformity to it."[v]

   According to Scofield's definition, in what ways are you living a life that is set apart from the world?

3. Paul begins his letter in Romans 1:2-3 by stating that the gospel of God was that "which He promised before through His prophets in the holy Scriptures. The gospel was not Paul's idea, nor was it an afterthought of God. It was promised before! What does Jesus declare about Himself in Luke 24:27 and Luke 24:44?

4. Look up and write out two verses from the Old Testament that point to and promise the coming of Christ.

5. The word *gospel* originates from the meaning of the New Testament Greek word *euaggelion* meaning, "A reward for good tidings, glad tidings of salvation through Jesus Christ, the proclamation of the grace of God made manifest in Jesus Christ, the gospel or good news of the words, deeds, life, death and the resurrection of Christ." *Strong's G2098, 2097.*

   Based upon your current knowledge of the gospel, why is it called *good news*?

6. In Romans 1:5, Paul expresses his desire to proclaim the gospel of Jesus Christ so that God's name would be exalted among all the nations of the world. Paul's special commission was to take the gospel to the Gentiles (the word nations means Gentiles), and this is why he was planning to go to Rome, the very capital of the empire. He was a preacher of the gospel, and the gospel was for all nations. In fact, Paul was anxious to go to Spain with the message of Christ (Romans 15: 28).[vi]

   Who in your sphere of influence, do you have the greatest opportunity of reaching with the gospel?

Day 2
Paul's Desire

Read Romans 1:8-15.

1. In Romans 1:11, we see the first mention of "spiritual gift" in the New Testament. Paul is longing to see the Roman believers in order to use his gifts to *establish* or *strengthen* them in their faith. Share a time that God used a sister to strengthen you in your faith.

2. Paul wrote to the Christians in Rome: "I am a debtor," and beginning with those words he describes the passion of his life. We know what it means to be debtors. Debt has become a way of life in our society. The national debt is something we hear about on the news daily. Personal debt has become a problem for many individuals and families. But here in Romans 1:14 it is not economic debt that's under consideration. It is spiritual, and it is the concept of obligation combined with passion! Paul considered himself obligated "to Greeks and to barbarians," and to the "wise and unwise." This obligation/passion was to preach the gospel. Paul's deep desire was to tell lost people the truth about Jesus Christ and instruct them in their response to Jesus Christ, to be saved from sin; to become Christians and have a faith that would influence many.[vii]

   Are you inspired or intimidated by Paul's excitement about preaching the gospel to the nations? Explain your answer.

3. According to verse 15, Paul was *ready* to preach the gospel. What are the commands of 2 Timothy 4:2 and 1 Peter 3:15?

4. In reference to 2 Timothy 4:2, Ray Stedman comments, "This word is not addressed to preachers only. It includes all the people of God, for Paul does not merely mean to preach; the word is really announce, proclaim, set it forth, deliver the truth, make it known. It is not something you argue about; you declare it because God Himself has said it. This can be done over a cup of coffee, in an office, or in a car while you are driving to work. It is something that can come up any place, any time. Where human hearts are open, seeking, longing, and hurting, there is the place, there is the opportunity to preach the word."[viii]

What do you think are some of the reasons many believers never share their faith?

5. When do you believe Christians are *ready* to share the gospel? Use Scripture to support your answer.

Day 3
Not Ashamed

Read Romans 1:16-17.

1. Fill in the blanks from Romans 1:16-17. These verses summarize the book's theme.

For I am not ashamed of the gospel of Christ, for it is the _____ of _____ to

_____ for everyone who believes, for the Jew first and also for the Greek.

For in it the _____ of God is revealed from faith to faith; as it is written, "The

_____ shall live by_____."

---

2. The word translated *ashamed* means *disgraced* or *personally humiliated.* Why would Paul be tempted to be ashamed of the gospel?

3. What are some practical ways a believer can move from being *ashamed* to being *excited* to share the gospel?

4. *The gospel is power.* The Greek word, which is translated *power* in Romans 1:16, is the word *dunamis.* From that Greek word we derive our English words *dynamite, dynamo,* and *dynamic.* "Dynamite is a destructive power, it blows things to pieces. A dynamo has constructive power. It produces energy. The gospel too tears down, it blows to pieces the old life. But at the same time it has the constructive power to build up the new life. It is absolutely true that the gospel is not only the dynamite of God but the dynamo too."[ix] What do you discover about the gospel's power from the following verses?

    *   Isaiah 55:11

- Jeremiah 23:29

- Ezekiel 36:26

- 2 Corinthians 10:4-5

- Hebrews 4:12

5. *The gospel is the power of God.* According to 1 Corinthians 1:24, "Christ is the power of God and the wisdom of God." Apart from Jesus Christ there is no gospel, there is no good news. Christ Himself is the good news. "The gospel of the crucified Christ is the power of God that rescues man from the dominion of sin and from divine judgment. The gospel is stronger than man's strength. People cannot rescue themselves from bondage to sin or its punishment by their own power. Human wisdom is unable to conquer "the wages of sin" (Romans 6:23), that is, death. Even so, the good news of Christ rescues and delivers. It overcomes even death (2 Timothy 1:10). Those who believe the gospel know the reality of its wisdom and power. For this reason, they exalt nothing above Christ and His saving work."[x]

According to 1 Corinthians 1:30, why should we glory in the Lord and the Lord alone?

6. *The gospel is the power of God to salvation.* Look up the word *salvation* in your glossary of terms and write a definition using your own words.

7. What additional truths do you learn about salvation from the following verses?

   - Acts 4:10-12

   - Romans 10:10

   - 2 Corinthians 7:10

   - Ephesians 1:13

   - Philippians 2:12

   - 1 Thessalonians 5:9

   - 2 Thessalonians 2:13

   - 2 Timothy 3:15

Day 4
The Righteousness of God

Read Romans 1:17.

1. In the gospel, the righteousness of God is revealed. Look up the word *righteousness* in your glossary of terms and write a definition using your own words.

2. What additional truths do you learn about righteousness from the following verses?

    - 1 Corinthians 1:30

    - 2 Corinthians 5:21

    - Ephesians 4:24

    - Philippians 3:9

    - 2 Timothy 3:16

    - Titus 3:5

    - 1 Peter 2:24

    - 1 John 3:10

3. In Romans 1:17, Paul is quoting from an Old Testament passage found in Habakkuk 2:4. It is mentioned two other times in the New Testament. According to Galatians 3:11 and Hebrews 10:38, what does it mean for "the just to live by faith?"

4. By the righteousness in the gospel, men and women are declared just in the eyes of God. It was Habakkuk—quoted by Paul in Romans 1:17—that ultimately shook Martin Luther to the core and brought him to saving faith in Jesus Christ. His youngest son, Dr. Paul Luther, wrote:

In the year 1544, my late dearest father, in the presence of us all, narrated the whole story of his journey to Rome. He acknowledged with great joy that, in that city, through the Spirit of Jesus Christ, he had come into the knowledge of the truth of the everlasting gospel. It happened this way. As he repeated his prayers on the Lateran staircase, the words of the prophet Habakkuk came suddenly to his mind, "The just shall live by faith." Thereupon he ceased his prayers, returned to Wittenberg, and took this as the chief foundation of all his doctrine. (Quoted in A Bunch of Everlastings, by Frank Boreham, pp. 19-20.)

From that unlikely beginning came the Protestant Reformation. And with it the battle cry Sola Fide, "by faith alone."

Sola Fide! = Faith Alone!

Faith alone! Not by works of the law.

Faith alone! Not by obedience to the Church.

Faith alone! Not by human righteousness.

Faith alone! Not by baptism.

Faith alone! Not by good intentions.

Faith alone! Not by the sacraments.

Faith alone! Not by acts of charity.

Faith alone! Plus nothing and minus nothing!

What does it mean to have "faith alone" in this sense? If you know what it means to believe a doctor when he says, "You need surgery," you know what it means to have faith. If you know what it means to step into an airplane entrusting your safety to the captain in the cockpit, you know what it means to have faith. If you know what it means to ask a lawyer to plead your case in court, you know what it means to have faith. Faith is complete reliance upon another person to do that which you could never do for yourself."[xi]

Take a moment to write your own SOLA FIDE! What does it mean to you to have faith alone to trust in God's righteousness and not your own?

Day 5
Reflection

The Wycliffe Bible Encyclopedia summarizes the gospel message this way: *The central truth of the gospel is that God has provided a way of salvation for men through the gift of His son to the world. He suffered as a sacrifice for sin, overcame death, and now offers a share in His triumph to all who will accept it. The gospel is good news because it is a gift of God, not something that must be earned by penance or by self-improvement.*

Millard Erickson in his book, *Christian Theology*, summarizes the gospel message this way: *Paul viewed the gospel as centering upon Jesus Christ and what God has done through Him. The essential points of the gospel are Jesus Christ's status as the Son of God, His genuine humanity, His death for our sins, His burial, resurrection, subsequent appearances, and future coming in judgment . . . that one is justified by faith in the gracious work of Jesus Christ in His death and resurrection. . . . [It is not] merely a recital of theological truths and historical events. Rather, it relates these truths and events to the situation of every individual believer.*

Before moving on in the Book of Romans, we want to make sure we have a solid understanding of the gospel and its definition. There are a few samples above to inspire you. Look up the following verses and write them out in your own words. Then, using your own words, write a gospel definition that you can easily share with others.

- John 3:16

- Romans 5:8-11

- 1 Corinthians 15:1-8

- Titus 2:11-14

MY GOSPEL DEFINITION

LESSON 1
Romans 1:1-17

Notes

LESSON 2: NO EXCUSES
The Judgment of God
Romans 1:18 – 3:20

LESSON 2
Romans 1:18 – 3:20

NO EXCUSES
The Judgment of God

LESSON 2 COMMENTARY

The idea of God's wrath in movies and in literature bring to mind the capricious destruction of people and property by storms, earthquakes, and mighty winds. In common parlance this destruction is described to be done to "biblical proportions," which describes their scope and the enormity of the destruction. While there is some of that, the reality is this notion misses the point. For it centers on how God's wrath is displayed, rather than why God has wrath.

What is God's wrath? Why does God have wrath? Alva McClain describes God's wrath as, "His holy aversion to all that is evil, and His purpose is to destroy it."[xii] God's wrath is revealed from heaven because men have held down the truth of what can be known about God. Why do men hold down the truth? We hold down the truth of God's word to supplant it with our own. It is this supplanting of God's truth for our own that has led to all of the violence and destruction that we see within the world.

Where did it all go wrong? Our parents, Adam and Eve chose to disobey the commands of almighty God, making them and all of their children (us) fundamentally marred by sin, unable to fulfill the commands of God, and subject to the reward for the deeds done in the flesh, which is death. Our consciences are marked by the effects of sin, everything we do bears the taint of sin, and our best efforts are saturated by the all-inclusive, permeating, and pervasive nature of sin. The reality dear friends is that man has become a horror, when compared to what God had intended him to be. We have become horrors to ourselves because we have rejected the truth of God and the truth about God. It is because we supplanted God's truth for our own and rejected His way, that man became evil and is subject to His wrath.

You might not be looking forward to studying two chapters dedicated to the topic of God's wrath, but unless we fully comprehend God's holiness and the justice of His anger, we will never fully understand or appreciate the greatness of His grace.

MEMORY VERSE

"For since the creation of the world His invisible attributes are clearly seen, being understood by the things that are made, even His eternal power and Godhead, so that they are without excuse (Romans 1:20).".

Day One
God's Wrath on Unrighteousness

"God's wrath is His holy hatred of all that is unholy. It is His righteous indignation at everything that is unrighteous. It is the temper of God towards sin. It is not God's uncontrollable rage, vindictive bitterness or a losing of His temper, but the wrath of righteous reason and holy law."[xiii]

Read Romans 1:18-32.

As powerful as the gospel is, there is one thing the gospel cannot do: it cannot save any man until that man sees himself as a guilty, lost, condemned sinner. Therefore, before Paul can even begin to talk about God saving sinners, he takes a large section of his letter to demonstrate why men need the gospel.

1. Romans 1:18a teaches us that "the wrath of God is revealed from heaven against all ungodliness and unrighteousness of men…" In two words, Paul sums up all of human sin, placing it in two great divisions.

UNGODLINESS

The Greek word used for ungodliness is *asébeia* which means "a lack of respect, showing itself in bold irreverence – i.e. refusing to give honor where honor is due (Strong's 763)." Ungodliness is a sin against the *being* of God. *An ungodly man lives as if there were no God.*

The book of Jude highlights the characteristics of the ungodly. What are they?

- Jude 1:4

- Jude 1:15-19

UNRIGHTEOUSNESS

The Greek word used for unrighteousness is *adikia* which means "the opposite of justice; unrighteousness, as a violation of God's standards (justice) which brings divine disapproval; a count (violation) of God's justice, i.e. what is contrary to His righteous judgments (what He approves). (Strong's G9) Unrighteousness is sin against the *will* of God. *An unrighteous man lives as if there were no will of God revealed.*

Describe unrighteousness according to Romans 1:29.

2. Romans 1:18b teaches "that men suppress the truth in unrighteousness." "Men suppress the truth because they take pleasure in unrighteousness. When you love sin, you cannot love the truth. The truth is too threatening. It threatens to take away your illicit pleasures. That is what unrighteousness is. Loving sin more than loving God and His truth.[xiv]

Provide some examples of things that we can be tempted to love more than God.

3. According to Romans 1:19-20, why are men *without excuse* as it relates to the knowledge of God?

4. Romans 1:21 teaches: Although men knew God …

   - **They did not glorify Him as God.** God made man to glorify Him. God's glory is the manifestation of His greatness. The purpose of creation is to glorify God and enjoy Him forever. People know enough about God to see that they should glorified Him as Creator, yet they withdraw their worship from Him. Give some examples of ways we withdraw our worship from God.

   - **They were not thankful.** 2 Timothy 3:2 speaks to people in the last days who are unthankful. Why is ungratefulness a danger to our spiritual lives?

   - **They became futile in their thoughts.** The Greek word *futile* carries the idea of *vain*, *vacuum*, or *void*. The idea is that empty and evil notions were sucked into men's minds to replace the notion of a Creator to whom they were responsible – this resulted in a pagan thought life. What additional insights do you gain regarding futile thinking in Ephesians 4:17-19?

- **Their foolish hearts were darkened.** By rejecting the knowledge of God in creation, people darken their hearts further. The problem with man is not that he is uneducated but that he hates God, hates His intrusion into his life. This hatred leads to a darkened soul towards God, the God who is the God of light. In biblical assumption man does not move upward. He has proclivity to devolve, not evolve. If he goes negative towards God, the pull of his heart is downward.[xv]

Describe some ways you can grow in love for God. Use Scripture to support your answer.

5. It was Charles Spurgeon who said, "Nothing teaches us about the preciousness of the Creator as much as when we learn the emptiness of everything else."[xvi] Paul shows us in Romans 1:22, 23, and 25 that idolatry is at the root of sin. People exchange the truth of God for the lie, and worship and serve the creature, rather than the Creator (v 25)."

Share a time that you placed your hope and trust in an idol. How did your idol disappoint you and leave you empty?

6. Our inward bent of sin creates such dysfunction and disorder that we defy the sovereign lordship of Christ, pursuing abnormal and unnatural relations as if they were natural and normal. What do you learn about homosexuality in Romans 1:26-27?

Day Two
God's Righteous Judgment

"God's love is an exercise of His goodness toward sinners. As such, it has the nature of grace and mercy. It is an outgoing of God in kindness which not merely is undeserved, but is actually contrary to desert; for the objects of God's love are rational creatures who have broken God's law, whose nature is corrupt in God's sight, and who merit only condemnation and final banishment from His presence."[xxvii]

Read Romans 2:1 – 2:5.

1. In the midst of many verses concerning God's judgment, Romans 2:4 appears like a breath of fresh air! Fill in the blanks from Romans 2:4.

Or do you _____ the riches of His _____ , _____ ,

and _____ , not knowing that the _____ of God

leads you to _____ ?

---

2. Paul highlights a beautiful truth; it is the goodness of God that leads us to repentance. God does not reveal His judgment to change hearts, He reveals His goodness. How does God reveal Himself to Moses in Exodus 34:6?

3. List the additional insights you learn about God's character in Joel 2:13 and 2 Peter 3:9.

4. Look up the word *despise* in a dictionary and write out the definition.

5. The Greek word for *repentance* is *metanoia*, which literally means a change of mind. It is a turning away from sin to God (Strong's 3341). What does Paul teach us about repentance in 2 Corinthians 7:10?

6. Because of God's kindness and long suffering, He has not yet judged unbelievers, giving them what they deserve. He is allowing them time to repent. His kindness and long suffering, extended to lost sinners, is meant to bring them to repentance. When unbelievers continue to despise God's goodness, "they are treasuring up wrath for themselves (Romans 2:5)." Believers can also despise the goodness of God by using it as a license to sin.

In what ways is the goodness of God causing you to be more Christ-like?

7. Why does it make sense that a hard and an unrepentant heart will be met with God's wrath, when His righteous judgment is revealed?

Day 3
Guilty as Charged

Read Romans 2:6-29.

1. Is it only some men who are evil? In Romans 1:18-2:29, Paul names three categories of people who are subject to the wrath of God.

   - The Pagan Man – The man who has never heard the gospel.
   - The Moral Man - The man who strives to live a good life.
   - The Religious Man – The man who keeps religious rules and regulations.

   According to Romans 3:10, what is the fourth all-inclusive category?

2. Paul writes about the hypocrisy of the religious and self-righteous Jews who thought because they knew the Law of Moses, they could win God's approval. In their condemnation of others, they excused and overlooked their own sins. Bible teacher Ray Pritchard comments, "Have you ever noticed how we like to "rename" our sins? We do that by ascribing the worst motives to others, while using other phrases to let ourselves off the hook."[xviii]

   > You lose your temper; I have righteous anger.
   > You're a jerk; I'm having a bad day.
   > You have a critical spirit; I bluntly tell the truth.
   > You gossip; I share prayer requests.
   > You curse and swear; I let off steam.
   > You're pushy; I'm intensely goal-oriented.
   > You're greedy; I'm simply taking care of business.
   > You're a hypochondriac; but I'm really sick.
   > You stink; I merely have an earthy aroma.

   Why is it dangerous for believers to adopt an, *I am better than you* mentality?

3. In verses 2:25-29, Paul speaks on the topic of circumcision. Look up the word *circumcision* in your glossary and using your own words, write a definition.

25

4. Romans 2:29 teaches us that circumcision is a matter of the heart. Paul argues that Jewish circumcision is only an outward sign of being set apart to God. However, if the heart is sinful, then physical circumcision is of no avail. An external religion is of no value at all: what counts is what is in our hearts.

   Read each of the following Scriptures, noting what you learn about circumcision.

   - Jeremiah 4:4

   - 1 Corinthians 7:19

   - Galatians 5:6

   - Philippians 3:3

   - Colossians 2:11

5. What are some ways in which you say one thing and do another?

Day 4
In Defense of God's Judgment

Read Romans 3:1-20.

1. We, like the Jewish people have been entrusted with the Word of God (Romans 3:2). The biblical knowledge we possess should make a difference in the way we live. What are some of the benefits of the Word of God according to Deuteronomy 4:5-9 and Psalm 19:7-11?

2. What responsibilities go along with being entrusted with God's Word and the gospel?

3. In Romans 3:3, Paul asks "What if some (Jews) did not believe? Will their unfaithfulness nullify God's faithfulness? Will the fact that some Jews sinned caused God to back out of His promises? What is the answer to Paul's question found in 2 Timothy 2:13?

4. How does Paul's describe our fallen condition in Romans 3:10-18?

5. The Jews may have proudly thought that Romans 3:10-18 applied to the Gentiles, but certainly not to them. Paul makes it perfectly clear in verse 19 that whatever the law says, it says to those who are under the law. No one will be declared righteous in God's sight by the works of the law. By the standard of the law we all fall short.

   What is the purpose of the law according to Romans 3:20?

Day 5
Reflection

1. Imagine a courtroom scene with God as the judge and the world on trial. From what you have learned in Romans 1:18-3:20, summarize the charges against us, the supporting evidence and the verdict.

2. Describe some of the thoughts and feelings you might have if you were on trial for committing a serious crime—and you knew you were guilty. Now consider the fact that Christ has set you free despite your guilt. How do you feel?

3. Have you fully embraced the fact that God has every right to judge you for your sins? Why or why not?

4. Are there any matters of the heart that you need to confess to God? Take a moment to write out a prayer of confession and ask God to help you live a life that is set apart to Him.

LESSON 2
Romans 1:18 – 3:20

Notes

LESSON 3: WHAT IS JUSTIFICATION?
Righteousness by Faith
Romans 3:21-4:25

LESSON 3
Romans 3:21-4:25

WHAT IS JUSTIFICATION?
Righteousness by Faith

LESSON 3 COMMENTARY

I have news for you. Do you want the bad news or the good news first? You can imagine it can't you? You've had your blood drawn, they've run the tests and the doctor calls you into the office to speak to you (they never give you information over the phone). You wait in the room, the doctor comes in and sits down. She asks you, "Do you want the good news or the bad news first?" The Apostle Paul gave us the bad news first. He told us that we are worse than sick. We are spiritually dead. We've all been struck with the blight of sin. Sin saturates every fiber of our being, and the sad fact is, there is no cure for it. The prognosis is eternal death and separation from God. No one is excluded, all of us have sinned and fallen short of God's glory (Romans 3:23). None of us are perfect. All of us deserve death.

These are stark and sobering truths that present a bleak picture. They are meant to. Our status before a holy God was death. The letter to the Romans could have ended with 3:20. God would be perfectly just to condemn us all and to leave us fearfully awaiting His wrath. "*But now* in Romans 3:21 marks a great transition. Those two words, *but now* make a great difference. They form a favorite expression with Paul. In his epistles he may at times paint the blackest picture possible and then say, *But Now*."[xix] Paul uses these words to transition from the *bad* news to the *good* news. The good news is that a "righteousness apart from the law has appeared, because it is God who justifies the believer by grace through faith." To justify means *to declare righteous*. The image is one of a court of law, where the judge declares the defendant *not guilty*. In this case, the defendant has placed her hope and faith in God. Acknowledging her inability to make herself righteous, she relies on the grace of God as her defense.

Justification is a declaration that means more than a not guilty verdict. In our country's criminal courts, a not guilty verdict may mean that there was not enough evidence to convict a person. Sometimes, even if a not guilty verdict is declared, it does not remove the stain of innuendo or take away the scandal that results from the criminal case. But with God, when He justifies the one who has faith in Him, it means that God who is the highest Judge in the highest court in the entire universe declares that person righteous. To the one who believes, that ought to bring great encouragement, and a new sense of worth and value. The guilt that we wrestle with has been adjudicated, the condemnation that we were under, taken away. We can celebrate with David when he declares, "Blessed is he whose transgression is forgiven, whose sin is covered (Psalm 32:1)."

MEMORY VERSE

"For what does the Scripture say? "Abraham believed God and it was accounted to him for righteousness (Romans 4:3)."

Day 1
God's Righteousness through Faith

"Now that Paul has proved all people are sinners, he sets out to explain how sinners can be saved. The theological term for this salvation is justification by faith. Justification is the act of God whereby He declares the believing sinner righteous in Christ on the basis of the finished work of Christ on the cross." [xx]

Read Romans 3:21-31.

1. Romans 3:23 sums up all of what we learned last week. Write the verse out in its entirety.

2. Look up the word *justification* in your glossary and using your own words write out what it means to be justified by faith.

3. Under the Old Testament law, righteousness came by people behaving, but under the gospel, righteousness comes by believing. What are some ways believers continue to attempt to justify themselves by their behavior?

4. Romans 3:25 teaches us that Jesus was our propitiation. Look up the word propitiation in your glossary. Using your own words, write out a definition.

5. According to Romans 3:24 -26, how can God be both just and the Justifier?

6. Paul is clear that salvation comes to us as a gift received by faith, not by works, but at the same time that God's commandments are not abolished. According to Romans 10:4, how does justification by faith uphold the law?

Day 2
Abraham Justified By Faith

Read Romans 4:1-12.

1. Read and write out Psalm 32:1-2.

2. Paul is quoting David in Romans 4:6-8. Paul demonstrates in these verses that David's righteousness, like Abraham's, was credited to him by faith. Are you surprised to learn that full forgiveness for sinners who trust in God was present even under the old covenant? Why or why not?

3. In Romans 4:9-11, what do you notice about the order of Abraham's faith and his circumcision? Which came first, his faith or his obedience? Why is this order important for the believer in Christ?

4. Look up the word *faith* in your glossary. What important truths do you learn about true biblical faith?

5. The world falsely believes that a person goes to heaven because of their good works. Celebrities and other people of status proudly announce their large donations to different charities, their assistance to orphans in third world countries, and a multitude of other good deeds. What does Isaiah 64:6 reveal about our righteous acts?

Day 3
The Promise Granted Through Faith

"It was not the fact that Abraham had meticulously performed the demands of the law that put him into his special relationship with God, it was his complete trust in God and his complete willingness to abandon his life to him."[xxi]

Read Romans 4:13-18.

1. According to Galatians 3:7, who are the children of Abraham?

2. It is true that the best commentary on the Bible is the Bible. Galatians 3:23-29 expounds on how we become God's children through faith. It also explains the connection to our father Abraham.

    Before the way of faith in Christ was available to us, we were placed under guard by the law. We were kept in protective custody, so to speak, until the way of faith was revealed. Let me put it another way. The law was our guardian until Christ came; it protected us until we could be made right with God through faith. And now that the way of faith has come, we no longer need the law as our guardian. For you are all children of God through faith in Christ Jesus. And all who have been united with Christ in baptism have put on Christ, like putting on new clothes. There is no longer Jew or Gentile, slave or free, male and female. For you are all one in Christ Jesus. And now that you belong to Christ, you are the true children of Abraham. You are his heirs, and God's promise to Abraham belongs to you (Galatians 3:23-29 NLT).

    Describe how these verses define the believer's inheritance.

    • Ephesians 1:11-14

    • 1 Peter 1:3-5

    • Revelation 21:7

34

3. What we have in Christ is being *kept* in heaven for us. Your crown of glory has your name on it. Although we enjoy many blessings as children of God here on earth, our true inheritance—our true home—is reserved for us in heaven. Like Abraham, we are "looking forward to the city with foundations, whose builder and maker is God" (Hebrews 11:10).

   Abraham lived looking forward to his future home. Find and write out 2 or 3 verses in the New Testament that teach us how to live with an eternal perspective.

4. What does 2 Corinthians 4:17 teach us about trials and troubles in this life?

5. Reflect on Romans 4:17 and the truth that God is the one who "calls things that are not as though they were." In what ways have you experienced this in your life?

Day 4
Unwavering Faith

Read Romans 4:19-25.

1. Both Abraham and Sara found a place in Hebrew's Hall of Faith. Read Hebrews 11:8-12 and cite the reasons they are rewarded for their faith.

2. Abraham did not consider his old and aging body (Romans 4:20-21). Instead, he did not waiver through unbelief but was strengthened in faith giving glory to God. He was fully convinced that what God has promised he was also able to perform. What truths about faith can you glean from Abraham's example?

3. 2 Corinthians 5:7 commands the believer to walk by faith and not by sight. What happens when a believer chooses to walk by sight?

4. *"The essence of Abraham's faith in this case was that he believed that God could make the impossible possible. So long as we believe that everything depends on our efforts, we are bound to be pessimists, for experience has taught the grim lesson that our own efforts can achieve very little. When we realize that it is not our effort but God's grace and power which matter, then we become optimists, because we are bound to believe that with God nothing is impossible."xxii*

   What situation are you currently facing that requires that you believe God can make the *impossible* possible?

5. Abraham's righteousness was imputed to him (Romans 4:23) and our righteousness is imputed to us (Romans 4:24). Through our faith in Christ, the righteousness of God is given to us. This is called *imputed* righteousness. To *impute* something is to ascribe or attribute something to someone. When we place our faith in Christ, God ascribes the perfect righteousness of Christ to our account so that we become perfect in His sight.[xxiii]

Describe the process of imputation found in 2 Corinthians 5:21.

Day 5
Reflection

1. How would your life be different if you had only the law to pursue in order to become righteous? How should faith change the way you live your life?

2. Take a moment to consider what you have learned this week? Are there any obstacles in your life that are stopping you from taking God at His Word and believing Him?

3. What are some ways you can grow in your confidence in God and trust in His promises?

4. Read the *Believing God* 5 Statement Pledge of Faith below. Circle any of the statements that highlight an area where you are struggling in your faith. Find a promise from Scripture that you can apply to increase your faith in that area. Write out your Scripture promise next to the statement you have circled.

THE BELIEVING GOD 5 STATEMENT PLEDGE OF FAITH

1. God is who He says He is.
2. God can do what He says He can do.
3. I am who God says I am.
4. I can do all things through Christ.
5. God's Word is alive and active in me.

LESSON 3
Romans 3:21-4:25

Notes

LESSON 4: PEACE WITH GOD
Adam vs. Christ
Romans 5:1-5:21

LESSON 4
Romans 5:1 - 5:21

PEACE WITH GOD
Adam vs. Christ

In Romans chapter 5, Paul uses parallelism to demonstrate the differences between the works of Adam, which brought condemnation and death to all of His children, to the work of Christ which brought reconciliation and life to the children of God. God's love is demonstrated in Christ's timely sacrifice for those who were helpless and undeserving of it. God provided the means of salvation, while Christ provided the way of salvation. The sacrifice of Christ for God's enemies is the grandest demonstration of mercy and grace that can be known.

Which one of us would lay down our own life for our enemy? Who would offer their own son as a sacrifice for his enemies? It is difficult to plumb the depths of God's love toward his enemies, but such is God's love.

The bishop of North Africa, St. Augustine, wrote of Adam saying, "He had a great grace, but it was a different kind, He was surrounded by the good things he received from His creator, goods which he had not matched by his merits, and he suffered no evil." He wrote further, "Adam was neither tried nor troubled by such strife and division of self against self; in that place of happiness he enjoyed peace with himself."[xxiv] In his sinless state Adam lacked nothing, and had everything he needed. He had a relationship with God. He walked with God. He did not suffer strife, or frustration, or inner angst. He had no problems or difficulties, yet, it was in that sinless state, that Adam sinned and brought death to all of his children. All of Adam's children live with a corrupted nature and are by nature enemies of God.

But peace with God came through the sacrifice of Jesus. Because Jesus died for sinners, satisfying the just wrath of God, believers can have peace with God. The Bible Knowledge Commentary writes, "God gave proof of His love by having Christ die in the place of humans "while we were still sinners."[xxv] Because of the sinner's response by faith to Christ's sacrifice on the cross, God has declared him righteous. Certainly that now-declared-righteous person will not be forsaken by God's love, which has been poured out effusively in his heart. Since the divine dilemma of justification has been solved on the basis of Jesus' shed blood, certainly Jesus Christ will see that justified sinners will be saved from God's wrath.

Because God treated His own Son in a way that he did not deserve, He can now treat us in a way that we do not deserve. Because of that we can rejoice and enjoy God.

MEMORY VERSE

Therefore having been justified by faith we have peace with God through our Lord Jesus Christ (Romans 5:1)."

Day 1
Faith Triumphs in Trouble

Read Romans 5:1-5.

1. According to Romans 5:1-5, what are some of the blessings believers enjoy now because they are justified by faith?

2. Believers enjoy both peace *with* God and the peace *of* God. What additional insights do you gain regarding the peace of God from Ephesians 2:14-18?

3. How is the Christian's definition of hope different from the definition of hope the world has adopted?

4. What do we learn about the benefits of suffering in Romans 5:3-4?

5. Tribulation produces perseverance. The Greek word for *tribulation* means "to abide under, or to stay under the pressure." Pressure is something we want to get out from under, but suffering teaches us to stay under, to stick in there and hang with it. How has your ability to persevere through trials changed since you first became a believer?

6. Perseverance produces character. The word *character* carries the idea of being proven or tested. What did Paul learn about God and suffering in 2 Corinthians 1:8-10?

7. Character produces hope. Our trials and tribulation serve to strengthen us. We can rejoice and rest assured that God is conforming us into the image of His Son. Consider a few of your most recent trials. Did you grow more Christ-like as a result? Why or why not?

8. Pastor Ray Stedman comments:

   Paul explains why our hope does not disappoint us. He says it is "because God has poured out His love into our hearts by the Holy Spirit, whom he has given us." Now, to my mind, this is one of the most important verses in the book of Romans. It is a very significant verse because it is adding a thought that we have not had in this book up to now. It is the explanation, above all else, of how to rejoice in suffering. You can see how important this is, because it is the first mention in the book of Romans of the Holy Spirit. This is also the very first time in this book that the love of God is brought in. Up to now, Paul has not said anything about the love of God, but now it is "the love of God that is shed abroad in our hearts, by the Holy Spirit, who is given to us."[xxvi]

   Do you see suffering through the lens of God's wrath or the lens of His love? Explain your answer.

Day 2
Christic in Our Place

Romans 5:-6-11.

1. What is your response to the deep and profound truths found in Romans 5:6-11? Write your response in the form of a short prayer to God.

2. According to Romans 5:6, 5:8, and 5:10, what were you like when Christ died for you?

3. When we were enemies of God, Christ loved us. How should this impact the way we relate to a lost and hurting world?

4. If we used to be God's enemies, and have been reconciled, what does that make us now? Use Scripture to support your answer. Write the verses out in their entirety.

5. How does God prove His love for you in Romans 5:8?

6. Take a moment to personalize Christ's death on the cross for your sins. How does your life reflect an attitude of gratitude for Christ's sacrifice on your behalf?

Day 3
Death in Adam, Life in Christ

"As sin and death entered the world through Adam, grace and life entered the world through Jesus. In this way, Jesus is the second (or "last") Adam (1 Corinthians 15: 45). This template, what is sometimes called "typology," is seen throughout the Old Testament. All of the heroes of the faith were stained by Adam's sin. Jesus, the sinless Redeemer of what Adam corrupted, is the truer and better Adam, the Prophet, Priest, and King that we all so desperately need." [xxvii]

Read Romans 5:12-17.

1. Based on the verses in Romans 5:12-17, highlight the differences between Adam and Christ.

2. Compare 1 Corinthians 15:20-22 with Romans 5:12-17.

3. Because of Adam's sin, believers were condemned (Romans 5:16). Look up the word *condemnation* in your glossary. Using your own words, describe what it means to be *condemned*.

4. What important truths do you learn about condemnation in John 3:17-18?

5. Believers in Jesus Christ will not face the condemnation of God. How do Colossians 2:15 and Hebrews 2:14-15 describe Christ's victory?

6. Share some of the victories you have had over sin in the course of your Christian walk.

Day 4
God's Great Grace

Read Romans 5:18-21

1. Look up the word *grace* in your glossary. Write a definition using your own words.

2. Romans 5:18 teaches us about "the free gift that came through one Man's righteous act." What additional information do you receive about this *free gift* in Ephesians 2:8-9?

3. What do you think Paul meant in Romans 5:20 when he said, "Where sin abounded, grace abounded much more?"

4. God is more ready to forgive then we are to sin. Are there any sins in your life that you are struggling to confess because you believe God's grace can't overcome them? Explain your answer.

5. What reasons has God's grace given you to rejoice, even during tough times?

Day 5
Reflection

In Paul Johansson's book, *Free by Divine Decree*[xxviii], he highlights a poem written by one of his students. Take time to read and reflect on what Gwen Thompson Eppert wrote. Journal your thoughts and include a prayer of love and gratitude to God for sending His precious Son.

All heaven and earth assembled, one dark and hopeless day,
As mankind stood before the judge, with nothing left to say,
There was a case against him, his verdict would be sealed,
Guilty without excuse, and no further appeal.
Silent, helpless, groping there man stood,
All evidence has been presented, his verdict now was sealed,
Guilty without excuse, and no further appeal.

Falling to his face in shame, without a word to say,
Man disclaimed the living God and followed his own way.
Before the case was laid to rest all gathered that day knew,
Man was guilty without excuse,
There was nothing he could do.

Fallen, prostrate there man lay, beneath the righteous chair,
Awaiting the dark sentence, he was now about to hear.
The evidence was conclusive, the courtroom held their breath,
When the judge slammed down his gavel,
The sentence would be death.

But to everyone's amazement, the gavel did not fall;
But One stood up with nail scarred hands and said,
"I paid it all."
I who knew no sin at all, became sin for thee,
And He held those nail-scarred hands outstretched,
For all the court to see.

All heaven in earth broke forth in praise,
That new and glorious day,
As mankind stood before the judge with nothing left to pay.
The case against him was dismissed, his pardon ever sealed,
Forgiven, loved, accepted in Christ his one appeal.

In man's darkest hour, Jesus came to embrace,
The utter degradation of Adam's helpless race,
My Lord who knew no sin at all, became sin for me,
That in His righteousness I'd stand for all eternity.

JOURNAL AND PRAYER

LESSON 4
Romans 5:1 - 5:21

Notes

LESSON 5: INSTRUMENTS OF RIGHTEOUSNESS
Dead to Sin, Alive to God
Romans 6:1-6:23

LESSON 5
Romans 6:1 – 6:23

INSTRUMENTS OF RIGHTEOUSNESS
Dead to Sin, Alive to God

What are you saying Paul? Are you saying that all I have to do is believe? Paul asks, "Why does that seem so strange?" Because, I have to be able to do something. It just doesn't seem right. I get chosen by God simply because I believed in Him? And if I sin, God's grace is revealed? A reasonable person would say, the more I sin, the more God's grace is revealed. I should sin more, so God's grace can be revealed more.

On the surface that seems like a fair assessment. If God's grace is revealed when we sin, we should sin more and in greater degrees so that God's grace could be revealed more and in greater degrees. This belief was called *antinomianism*, which Merriam-Webster defines as one who holds that under the gospel dispensation of grace the moral law is of no use or obligation because faith alone is necessary to salvation. Paul responds emphatically, "Certainly Not!" He states, we died to sin, how can we live in it any longer? Living in sin is like getting ready to go to the prom. You travel to the manicurist to get your nails polished. You pay a fortune at the hair salon to get your hair styled. You hire a make-up artist. Now, after putting on your expensive prom dress, imagine going outside and rolling around in the mud! Who would do such a thing?

Thomas Constable writes, "Note that Paul did not say that it is impossible to live in sin or that sin is dead to the Christian (i.e., that it no longer appeals to us). He meant it is unnecessary and undesirable to live in sin, to habitually practice it."[xxix]

Instead, Paul tells us we ought to reckon ourselves dead to sin. "The word reckon is a word for faith—in the face of appearances."[xxx] Reckoning ourselves dead to sin is an important step for the believer. When the believer completely identifies with the death, burial, and resurrection of Christ, she understands that Christ's actions changed her relationship with sin forever. Because Christ died for her sins, she died to sin, and in dying to sin, her relationship to sin is forever changed. The fact that we are united with Christ in his death, burial, and resurrection changes our relationship to sin. This change in our relationship to sin signifies that sin should no longer have dominion or power over us. In reckoning ourselves dead to sin, it does not mean that we shall be free from sin, it means that sin's power to dominate us has been broken forever. Now it is up to us (an act of our wills) with the aid of the Holy Spirit (who is alive and active in us), to live like people who are no longer subject to sins domination.

MEMORY VERSE

"Likewise you also, reckon yourselves to be dead indeed to sin, but alive to God in Christ Jesus our Lord (Romans 6:23)."

Day 1
Newness of Life

Read Romans 6:1-10.

1. A continuing lifestyle of unrestrained sin is inconsistent with our identity as believers. The person we used to be, a person in slavery to sin, has died. We now have a new life, one which comes from Christ and frees us from sin's control. Therefore, our lives should reflect this new reality. Paul presents a great question in Romans 6:1, "Shall we continue in sin that grace may abound?" Why or why not?

2. In Romans 6:3, 6, and 9 Paul uses the word "know" three times. Warren Wiersbe comments, "Paul wanted us to understand a basic doctrine. Christian living depends on Christian learning; duty is always founded on doctrine. If Satan can keep a Christian ignorant, he can keep him impotent." [xxxi]

   What are believers commanded to do in 2 Timothy 2:15 and why is learning what we believe so vital to our living it out?

3. *"Historians agree that the mode of baptism in the early church was immersion. The believer was "buried" in the water and brought up again as a picture of death, burial, and resurrection. Baptism by immersion (which is the illustration Paul is using in Romans 6) pictures the believer's identification with Christ in His death, burial, and resurrection. It is an outward symbol of an inward experience. Paul is not saying that their immersion in water put them "into Jesus Christ," for that was accomplished by the Spirit when they believed. Their immersion was a picture of what the Spirit did: the Holy Spirit identified them with Christ in His death, burial, and resurrection."* [xxxii]

   If baptism is merely a symbol, is it necessary for Christians? Why or why not? Share your baptism experience. If you have not been baptized, are you ready to take that step? Why or why not?

4. Paul teaches us in Romans 6:5 that our union with Christ assures our future resurrection from death. Romans 6:4 teaches us that we can benefit from that same resurrection power *now in order to walk in newness of life!* That means our former life, prior to salvation died. Our new life in Christ should be free from all the sinful and corrupt habits of the old life. The new life is a pursuit of heavenly things, not earthly things.

    Write out 2 Corinthians 5:17. How is your life different now then it was before you were saved? Have you put your past behind you, why or why not?

Day 2
Instruments of Righteousness

Read Romans 6:11-14.

1. As a result of the victory Christ has won over sin and death, we now have a choice. We can continue to allow sin to control us, even though it no longer has any legitimate authority over us. Or we can choose to offer ourselves and our bodies to God for His use as "instruments of righteousness". To continue to serve sin would be like a slave, having been freed from a wicked master after the Civil War, voluntarily continuing to obey that master.

    What have you found to be helpful in resisting sin in your life? Use Scripture to support your answer.

2. According to Romans 6:11, believers are to *reckon* themselves to be dead. Because Christ died in our place, we are dead to the power of sin.

    Pastor James McDonald paints a great picture, "It's as if we used to live in an apartment with an awful landlord who would burst in whenever he wanted, but now we've moved to a new apartment with a new landlord. We have new locks; we owe the former landlord nothing. He can't get into our new apartment unless we open the door and invite him in. Unfortunately, some Christians still open that door and listen to the old landlord. But he's no longer in control. In Christ, the power of sin is broken and defeated. Sin is not in charge. You have a new Master. Whether you feel dead to it or not doesn't matter. If you exercise your faith, you will experience victory. Believe in your heart and confess with your mouth, "I'm dead to that." Your behavior, speech, attitudes—whatever you are working on—will be increasingly changed"[xxxiii]

    Fill in the blank with any areas of sin in your life that you seek to have victory over.

    I'm dead to _____.

    I'm dead to _____.

    I'm dead to _____.

3. Give some practical ways we can present our members as instruments of righteousness.

4. *Reckon* is an accounting term. It means to *count, compute, calculate, or count over*. "Do you "do the math" when it comes to your relationship with Jesus? To use a bank account well, you have to understand some basic concepts like addition and subtraction and that spending takes money out. You have to realize that the amount in the bank is real regardless of how you feel. You have to spend time checking what is in your account. And you have to intentionally connect your actions to what is in the account. Do you understand basic concepts about the cross, atonement, forgiveness and what Christ has done? Do you think about, read about, and meditate on these realities? Do you spend time thinking about what is in your Christ account? Do you live by what you *feel* to be true, or do you live by what is really true? And do you connect your life to the life of Christ? The right actions in your life are never going to be produced if you do not start with the right thinking. Freedom comes to those who "do the math" when it comes to who they are in Christ."[xxxiv]

Are you doing the math when it comes to who you are in Christ? Are you living by how you feel, or what you know to be true? Explain your answer.

Day 3
Slaves of Righteousness

"The generic meaning of sanctification is "the state of proper functioning." To sanctify someone or something is to set that person or thing apart for the use intended by its designer. A pen is "sanctified" when used to write. Eyeglasses are "sanctified" when used to improve sight. In the theological sense, things are sanctified when they are used for the purpose God intends. A human being is sanctified, therefore, when he or she lives according to God's design and purpose."xxxv

Read Romans 6:15-18.

1. The master/slave relationship is used several times in the New Testament to describe the relationship between God and His people. What important truth do we learn about this relationship in Luke 16:13?

2. Why is it impossible to serve two masters? Who is your master?

3. The result of a believer's faith is their sanctification. Paul uses these verses to describe our part in sanctification. Christ sanctifies us with His blood, washing away our sins, but it is up to us to cleanse ourselves, put away sin and cling to the Word of God. We are to set ourselves apart from sin and unto righteousness. What are believers instructed to do in 2 Corinthians 7:1 and 1 Peter 1:14-16?

4. According to Romans 6:17, we can thank God that "though we were slaves of sin, we obeyed from the heart that form of doctrine to which we were delivered (the gospel)." The phrase "became obedient from the heart" is important. Paul's point is that God works His salvation in a person's innermost being, changing the heart of every sinner who places their trust in Christ's finished work on Calvary. A believer's obedience is not forced or legalistic, a believer obeys because they are willing. The corollary is that a person whose heart has not been changed and does not possess this desire to obey has not been saved.

   How do you know that your heart has been changed by the gospel?

5. No outward obedience is of the slightest value unless the heart turns to God. What important truth do we learn from 1 Samuel 16:7?

Day 4
Eternal Life

Read Romans 6:19-23.

1. Our lives before Christ produced fruit that made us ashamed. Give some examples of fruit that made you ashamed.

2. Our new lives in Christ produce fruit that glorifies God and brings joy to our lives. Give some examples of fruit in your life that glorifies God and brings you joy.

3. For those who have become slaves of God, they have the fruit of holiness, and at the end of their lives everlasting life. What do you learn about eternal life from the following verses?

   - John 6:68

   - John 10:28

   - John 17:3

   - 1 Timothy 6:12

   - 1 Timothy 6:19

   - Titus 1:2

   - Titus 3:7

4. Read Matthew 6:19-21. Are you laying up treasures in heaven or here on earth? Explain your answer.

5. In Colossians 3:2, we are instructed to "set our minds on things above, not on things on the earth." Share some ways believers can practically obey this command.

Day 5
Reflection

"For sin shall not have dominion over you, for you are not under law but under grace (Romans 6:14)." In Paul's mind, law and grace are incompatible. One brings slavery and death, the other brings freedom. Using the following chart for reference, check off the areas in your life where you are walking by the law, or walking by grace *(Adopted from Tim Keller's Gospel Curriculum.)*

LAW (RELIGION)	GRACE (GOSPEL)
I obey, therefore I am accepted.	I'm accepted, therefore I obey.
Motivation is based on fear and insecurity.	Motivation is based on grateful joy.
I obey God in order to get things from God.	I obey God to get God – to delight in Him and resemble Him.
When circumstances in my life go wrong, I'm angry at God, or myself, since I believe that anyone who is good deserves a comfortable life.	When circumstances in my life go wrong, I struggle, but I know all my punishment fell on Jesus, and while that God may allow this for my training, He will exercise His Fatherly love within my trial.
When I am criticized, I am furious or devastated, because it is critical that I think of myself as a "good person". Threats to that self-image must be destroyed at all costs.	When I am criticized, I struggle, but it is not essential for me to think of myself as a "good person." My identity is not built on my record or performance but on God's love for me in Christ.
My prayer life consists largely of petition, and it heats up only when I am in a time of need. My main purpose in prayer is control of the environment	My prayer life consists of generous stretches of praise and adoration. My main purpose is to fellowship with God.
My self-view swings between two poles, If and when I am living up to my standards, I feel confident but then I am prone to be proud and unsympathetic to failing people. If and when I am not living up to standards, I feel humble but not confident, I feel like a failure.	My self-view is not based on my moral achievement. In Christ I am *simul istus et peccator* – simultaneously sinful and lost, yet accepted in Christ. I am so bad that He had to die for me, and I am so loved that He was glad to die for me. This leads me to deep humility and confidence at the same time.
My identity and self-worth are based mainly on how hard I work, or how moral I am, and so I must look down on those I perceive as lazy or immoral.	My identity and self-worth are centered on the One who died for me. I am saved by sheer grace, so I can't look down on those who believe or practice something different from me. Only by grace I am what I am.

LESSON 5
Romans 6:1 – 6:23

Notes

LESSON 6: FREED FROM THE LAW
The Problem of the Flesh
Romans 7:1-7:25

LESSON 6
Romans 7:1 – 7:25

FREED FROM THE LAW
The Problem of the Flesh

When you reflect on your childhood, you are able to recognize a series of changes in your relationship with your parents. Depending on your parents, the way they ruled over you differed according to your age. When you became an adult, their rule over you completely changed. Your parent's temporary rule over your life served its purpose. Likewise, the Mosaic Law served its purpose. It shepherded the people until Christ came. Now that it had served its purpose, the people were no longer obligated to keep it. The Jew had radically identified themselves with the Law of Moses, making Paul's words not only difficult to hear, but difficult to receive. Paul has already argued that the Law of Moses could not justify the believer. Now he is articulating the believer's new relationship to the Law.

The Law had a good purpose and worked in the way that it was intended. But now, it cannot help us in our goal of sanctification. Since the believer has been declared righteous, having been justified by God, she now has to be made righteous through sanctification. Some scholars call that process of sanctification, progressive or experiential. In either case, it is the process by which God practically makes the believer what she is positionally. Paul Enns describes it this way, "Although the believer's positional sanctification is secure, her experiential sanctification may fluctuate because it relates to her daily experience."[xxxvi] Look at it this way, God has already anchored you to Himself so that your daily struggle with sin cannot dislodge you from Whom you are anchored to. The anchor is strong because God made it, our struggles with sin do not have the ability to tear us away from God.

This was accomplished by our new status, not by our own hand, nor by the law. The law was only capable of showing us how bad we are. Sin made use of the law (which was good) to produce death. The law possessed no ability whatsoever to make us righteous, being children of Adam marked us as guilty. The law confirmed that Adam's sin had passed on to each of us and sin used it to kill all of Adam's children. The law had no positive ability to make those who kept it righteous. Being sinners by nature, it became impossible to keep the law, leaving man in a dilemma. The law was good and man was by nature a law breaker. But God wiped out the written code that was against us and placed something better in its place.

This is why understanding our struggle with sin is important. Paul knew that being in Christ the Christian is freed from sin's domination. But here he reminds us that being free from sin's domination, does not mean that we are free from sin's strong attraction. This explains how we can intellectually despise a behavior, but willfully approve the thing we despise. When we are hurt by someone, we know that vengeance is God's to repay, but in the depths of our hearts we actively pursue vengeance ourselves. Constable writes, "Intellectually Paul argued that he should obey the Mosaic Law (vs.22), but morally he found himself in rebellion against what he knew was right (vs.23). This natural rebelliousness was something he could not rid himself of (vs. 24)."[xxxvii] Paul finds that the solution to this dilemma is not in denying that the problem exists or escaping into legalism, but it is through victory over sin, by faith in the finished work of Christ.

MEMORY VERSE
"O wretched man that I am! Who will deliver me from this body of death (Romans 7:24)?"

Day 1
Freed From the Law

Read Romans 7:1-6.

What really is legalism? It is the belief that I can become holy and please God by obeying laws. It is measuring spirituality by a list of dos and don'ts. The weakness of legalism is that it sees sins (plural) but not sin (the root of the trouble). It judges by the outward and not the inward. Furthermore, the legalist fails to understand the real purpose of God's law and the relationship between law and grace.[xxxviii]

1. How does Paul use the example of marriage to illustrate our freedom from the law?

2. The believer in Christ has become dead to the law through Christ's death. The believer becomes alive in Christ through His resurrection and is now married to Christ. The believer is joined to Christ and in union with Him. It is a love relationship, not a legal one. It is not religion or a set of rules or a system of morality. It is the enjoyment of an intimate and abiding relationship with God through Jesus Christ whom He sent.

   Have you been living in a love relationship with God or a legal one? Explain your answer.

3. Fill in the blanks from Romans 7:6.

But now we have been _____ from the _____, having died

to what we were held by, so that we should _____ in the newness of the

_____ and not in the oldness of the letter.

---

4. According to Romans 7:6, what is it that we have died to through the death of Christ, and for what purpose?

5. Compare Romans 7:6 with Galatians 2:20.

64

Day 2
The Problem with the Law

Read Romans 7:7-12.

1. Warren Wiersbe commented, "Something in human nature wants to rebel whenever a law is given."[xxxix] Why do think this is part of our human nature?

2. According to James 1:22-25, how does the law serve as a mirror?

3. Why do you think Paul used the sin of coveting in Romans 7:7 to make his point, instead of the other 10 commandments like, stealing, adultery or murder?

4. Paul makes it clear that when we try to live by rules and regulations, it only arouses more sin in us and creates more problems in our lives. How have you found this to be true in your own life?

5. Read Galatians 3:1-3. What problem in the Galatian church is Paul addressing?

Day 3
The Law is Powerless to Save

Read Romans 7:13-23.

"Our nature is carnal (fleshly), but the law's nature is spiritual. This explains why the old nature responds as it does to the law. It has well been said, "The old nature knows no law, the new nature needs no law." The law cannot transform the old nature; it can only reveal how sinful that old nature is. The believer who tries to live under law will only activate the old nature; he will not eradicate it."[xl]

1. Was there ever a time in your life prior to trusting Christ when you tried to "turn over a new leaf," to change your life for the better? How did it turn out?

2. Look up the word *flesh* in your glossary. Write a definition using your own words. Also, include what you learn about the *carnal* Christian.

3. What additional insight can you gain from Galatians 5:16-18 as it relates to the verses you are studying today?

4. If you could ask a dozen New Testament scholars to list the five most difficult passages in the New Testament, most would include Romans 7:14-25 on their list. "How can the regenerate Paul—man of God that he is, and author of Romans 6 and 8—be experiencing such a struggle with sin as we see in Romans 7?" J. I. Packer offers a key insight:

    "Paul wasn't struggling with sin because he was such a sinner. Paul was struggling because he was such a saint. Sin makes you numb. People who sin over and over again become desensitized to sin. The reason Paul's "struggle" was so intense was not because he was caught in a web of sin, or because he thought of himself as hopelessly doomed to giving into the temptations that he faced. Rather, it was because Paul lived a life so sensitive to the Holy Spirit and passionate about the glory of God that he intensely felt his sins whenever he became aware that he had committed a sin (since he was not, of course, sinlessly perfect)."[xli]

    Is your struggle with sin because you are sensitive to the Holy Spirit and want to live righteously for God, or are you struggling with sin because you have become desensitized to it? Explain your answer.

Day 4
Thank God!

Read Romans 7:24-25.

"Oh, what a miserable person I am! Who will free me from this life that is dominated by sin and death? Thank God! The answer is in Jesus Christ our Lord. So you see how it is: In my mind I really want to obey God's law, but because of my sinful nature I am a slave to sin (Romans 7:24-25 NLT)."

1. What is the only way a believer can escape the predicament described in this chapter?

2. As a faithful teacher, the apostle Paul in Romans 7:14–25 uses his own experiences and what he has learned through them to teach other believers how to use God's provision and our position in Christ to overcome the struggle with our carnal nature. How should our position in Christ inform how we live for Christ?

3. One day believers will be completely freed from the body of death in which we live when we are glorified with Christ in heaven, but until that day we rely on the power of the Spirit who indwells us and gives us victory in the ongoing battle with sin. Our key to victory in our struggle with sin lies in the very promise of God Himself. What is God's promise to us in 1 Corinthians 10:13?

4. Provide an example of a practical application from 1 Corinthians 10:13.

Day 5
Reflection

1. Romans 7 shows us who we were and who we are now. A Christian is both a saint and a sinner. How should the believer in Christ live in the tension of these two realities?

2. Reflect on what you have learned this week. Consider if there might be any area of your walk with Christ where you have allowed legalism to creep in. Record the simplicity of the Psalmist's words of encouragement in Psalm 37:3-5.

3. 1 John 3:24 reads, "Now he who keeps His commandments abides in Him, and He in him. And by this we know that He abides in us, by the Spirit whom He has given us." How can Paul assert that we are free to stop sinning and to start obeying? Because we are united with God's own Son. Obedience from our heart, not unopposed, is now natural to us. Using 2 Corinthians 5:14-15, describe Paul's motivation to live for Christ.

LESSON 6
Romans 7:1 – 7:25

Notes

LESSON 7: INSEPARABLE LOVE

Life in the Spirit
Romans 8:1-8:39

LESSON 7
Romans 8:1 – 8:39

INSEPARABLE LOVE
Life in the Spirit

After being set free from the demands of the law, we are no longer under the condemnation that the law brings. How has this been accomplished? Jesus paid the penalty, suffering death because we could not. We who believe have been set free! But how does a freed woman celebrate her freedom? Does she yoke herself to the same activities that exemplified her bondage? Paul would say, "Certainly not!" But many people who are free still live with the emotional and psychological effects of sin that result in an overwhelming sense of guilt.

When Paul declares in Romans 8:1, "There is therefore now no condemnation to those who are in Christ Jesus, who do not walk according to the flesh," he is telling us that since Christ has taken away the condemnation, the thing that really made us guilty, our feelings of guilt no longer have a basis in reality.

The New American Commentary puts it this way, "The good news Paul declared is that not only has the condemnation of the law (objective guilt) been removed but also that all our subjective guilt has no further basis in reality. We need not go through life carrying the heavy burden of sorrow for sins that already have been forgiven."[xlii] Athletes offer us a unique example: when an athlete suffers a major injury, they go get surgery and spend months rehabilitating the injury. After their rehabilitation is finished there is a period of time where the athlete has to psychologically move past the injury. They have to trust in the work that the surgeon has done in order to play the game without fear of re-injuring themselves. The sooner they move past the psychological effects, they are able to resume their careers.

Through the death and sacrifice of Jesus, God has healed us. God determined that He would do this beforehand. He has wiped out the code that was written against us, so that, we could be free from guilt and condemnation. Free to actually live for Him and free to experience and enjoy Him forever!

MEMORY VERSE

Nor height nor depth, nor any other created thing, shall be able to separate us from the love of God which is in Christ Jesus our Lord (Romans 8:39)."

Day 1
No Condemnation

Read Romans 8:1-11.

Romans 8 summarizes and drives home to the human heart the implications of our salvation presented in Romans 1– 7 and prepares the way for Paul to discuss the relationship between Jews and Gentiles in God's plan (Romans 9–11, 15) and the practical outworking of life in the Spirit (Romans 12– 14).

1. Look up the word *Spirit* in your glossary. Write a definition that includes what it means to walk in the Spirit.

2. Refresh your memory by looking up the word *condemnation* in your glossary. What is your response to the truth that, "There is no condemnation to those who are in Christ Jesus (Romans 8:1)?"

3. Explain the difference between *condemnation* and *conviction*. Why is it important that believers are able to distinguish between the two?

4. Condemnation is used by the enemy to remind us of our past faults and failures, to the point that we become spiritually debilitated, and utterly defeated. Describe the remedy to condemnation found in 1 John 3:20-21.

5. What are some practical ways to set your mind on the things of the Spirit (Romans 8:5)?

Day 2
Sonship through the Spirit

Read Romans 8:12-17.

1. Open your Bible and read through Romans 8 in its entirety. Circle all of the references to the *Spirit*. What does this reveal to you about the role of the Spirit for those who are no longer under the law? According to John 14:25-26, and John 16:5-16, what are some of the things the Holy Spirit does for the believer in Christ?

2. What evidence do you see of your life being controlled by the Spirit?

3. Share some characteristics of the person whose mind is set on the flesh.

4. Look up the word *adoption* in your glossary. Write a definition that includes what it means to be adopted into the family of God.

5. List the privileges and responsibilities of the child of God found in 1 John 2:28-3:3.

6. David Wilkerson describes how the Holy Spirit bears witness with our spirit that we are children of God, "The Holy Spirit presents you to the Father. And he keeps reminding you, "I have sealed the papers. You are no longer an orphan—you are legally a son of God! You now have a very loving, wealthy, powerful Father. Embrace him—call him 'my Father.' I have come to show you how much you're loved by him! He loved and wanted you!"[xliii]

   Are you often reminded by the Holy Spirit of God's love for you? How so?

Day 3
From Suffering to Glory

Read Romans 8:18-30.

1. In these verses, Paul desires that we would make it our aim to face suffering in light of the God we serve and the glorious person He's making us to be. Believers in Christ do not suffer without purpose. God has glory in mind. In what ways does God use suffering to conform us into His image? Use Scripture to support your answer.

2. According to Romans 8:26-27, we are victorious over suffering when we turn to prayer in the Holy Spirit. What does the Spirit do to help us in our time of trial?

3. We win over suffering when we embrace it for the good God has ordained will come from it (Romans 8:28). God takes not only the good things that happen, but He takes all things and works them for the ultimate benefit of those who love him. What is the testimony of Joseph in Genesis 50:20?

4. Describe a time God took something bad that happened to you and worked it for your good.

5. "We are told that God has not only a short-term, but also an eternal purpose for our lives. Ultimately, this purpose is to become a person who has been transformed to be like Jesus Christ. This path to our own glorification has been made for us, beginning in God's foreknowledge of all things. He knew us before time began. He knew we would respond to His call to salvation by grace through faith in Christ. In that sense, God has already "predestined" us to be "glorified;" that within the unique individuals we are, we will be perfectly expressed in and through the perfection of who Jesus Christ is. It is this ultimate glory that awaits us that we find to be our ultimate strength through suffering. We will be with Him forever and be just like Him by His love and grace."[xliv]

   If you knew you were going to win a football game, how would you play even if you were behind, sore, and tired? Now describe how to apply that principle to the suffering of this life.

Day 4
God's Everlasting Love

Read Romans 8:31-39.

1. "What shall we say to these things (Romans 8:31)?" Paul's comments are based upon not only what he has summarized in v. 29-30, but the entire book up until now. What do you say to these life changing things you have learned up to this point?

Paul continues in this chapter by answering five questions that will inevitably come up as a believer faces the suffering of life in a fallen world. The answers to these five questions provide a powerful framework of truth that can overcome some of Satan's most powerful tactics in his effort to drag us back into defeat and bondage to sin.

2. Romans 8:31 asks, "If God is for us, who can be against us?" Do you believe that God is for you? In what ways do the following scriptures prove it?

- Psalm 36:5

- Psalm 86:15

- Isaiah 54:17

- Jeremiah 29:11

- Zephaniah 3:17

- Matthew 6:26

- John 15:13

- 1 John 4:9-10

3. "How shall He not freely give us all things (Romans 8:32)?" God will bring us to ultimate victory. Paul draws upon the logical conclusion that if God gave Himself, in the person of Christ, He will obviously give all of the lesser things needed to accomplish the completion of our salvation and calling. What are some of those things God has given you to walk in victory? Use Scripture to support your answer.

4. "Who shall bring a charge against God's elect (Romans 8:33)?" Being in Christ, there is no foe that can lay a charge against us. Demonstrate from Romans 8:26, 31, and 34 how all three Persons of the Godhead are involved in our victory.

6. Who is he who condemns (Romans 8:34)? Matthew Henry comments:

   "By the merit of His death He paid our debt. Yea, rather that is risen again. This is convincing evidence that Divine justice was satisfied. We have such a Friend at the right hand of God; all power is given to him. He is there, making intercession. Believer! Does your soul say within you, Oh that He were mine and oh that I were His; that I could please Him and live to Him! Then do not toss your spirit and perplex your thoughts in fruitless, endless doubtings, but as you are convinced of ungodliness, believe on Him who justifies the ungodly. You are condemned, yet Christ is dead and risen. Flee to Him as such."[xlv]

   What were Jesus' words to the woman caught in adultery in John 8:10-11?

7. "Who shall separate us from the love of Christ (Romans 8:35)?" Paul is careful to include many facets of suffering, so his readers may know that no matter the trial, "in all these things we are more than conquerors through Him who loved us (Romans 8:37)."

   - Tribulation - A term for intense pressure that conveys the thought of problems and troubles pressing in upon a person from all sides.

   - Distress - This word is composed of two Greek words: "stenos" which means narrow, and "chora" which means space. This would refer to the person who is confined, restricted by outside circumstances

   - Persecution -This refers to relentless pursuit by another with the intent to harm.

   - Famine - Paul uses this term to refer to the shortage of food that may result from natural causes or financial loss.

- Nakedness - This refers to a person who was unable to purchase appropriate clothing, not to literal nakedness.

- Peril - This refers to dangers from various sources including political and criminal as well as various natural dangers resulting from traveling in ancient times.

In this life it will actually be God's love poured into our inner being that will strengthen us and give us the faith to conquer unbelief, sin, and rebellion against God under any situation. What are some practical ways we can stop believing that God has forsaken us when we go through great suffering?

Day 5
Reflection

1. Read 1 Samuel 17:33-50. What do you learn from David's example as it relates to facing the *giants* in your life?

2. Read Daniel 3:16-25. Shadrach, Meshach and Abednego did not know *how* God would choose to *deliver* them, but they were confident He *would deliver* them. Are you confident of God's deliverance? Why or why not?

3. When did you begin to realize that God loves you, that He is on your side, and that He does not condemn you, but wants to save you?

4. In your own words, write a paragraph or two, explaining why, "nothing shall be able to separate *you* from the love of God which is in Christ Jesus (Romans 8:39)."

LESSON 7
Romans 8:1 – 8:39

Notes

LESSON 8: ISRAEL'S REJECTION
A Burden for the Lost
Romans 9:1-33

LESSON 8
Romans 9:1 – 9:33

ISRAEL'S REJECTION
A Burden for the Lost

Paul's letter is written out of a deep concern for his people. Paul's burden is for those who are lost because of their rejection of the gospel. Evidence of his burden is reflected in vs. 3, "For I could wish that I myself were accursed from Christ for my brethren, my countrymen according to the flesh." This is an incredible statement of love. Who except someone with a deep love for the lost would conceive of thinking such a thing? Can you imagine loving someone so much that you might be willing to be separated from Christ so that they can be saved? Paul's anguish is similar to that of Moses, who anguished over the Jews because they turned to idols of gold rather than God.

In the Exodus account, Moses goes to the Lord for the sake of the Jews, "Now it came to pass on the next day that Moses said to the people, "You have committed a great sin. So now I will go up to the Lord; perhaps I can make atonement for your sin." Then Moses returned to the Lord and said, "Oh, these people have committed a great sin, and have made for themselves a god of gold! Yet now, if You will forgive their sin—but if not, I pray, blot me out of Your book which You have written. "And the Lord said to Moses, "Whoever has sinned against Me, I will blot him out of My book" (Exodus 32:30-33). Moses' heart was torn because he loved his people, they had sinned against God, but Moses did not want to see them cut off for their sins. Paul's anguish was the same. He had a tremendous burden for the Jewish people. He knew that God had good intentions toward His people and that their rejection would end in eternal separation. Paul was passionate that they would come to know the truth about the way to righteousness.

Similarly, our passion for the lost must be stirred. The lost are not here to be destroyed, God desires that they be saved. Acts 17:26-27 reads, "And He has made from one blood every nation of men to dwell on all the face of the earth, and has determined their preappointed times and the boundaries of their dwellings, so that they should seek the Lord, in the hope that they might grope for Him and find Him, though He is not far from each one of us." Constable writes, "God's purpose in regulating times and boundaries was that people would realize His sovereignty and seek Him (cf. Romans 1; John 6:44; 12:32). God, Paul said, is not far from human contact."[xlvi] God's intent is that people find Him, not reject Him. Their responsibility is to respond to God's kind extension of His grace and mercy through Jesus Christ.

Love and anguish must dislocate our heart from its comfortable setting. Great sorrow in the heart over the lost must move the believer to action. She must say, "I cannot stand by and do nothing! I must speak!"

MEMORY VERSE

"What then shall we say then, is there unrighteousness with God? Certainly not (Romans 9:14)!"

Day 1
A Heart for the Lost

Read Romans 9:1-5.

In the first eight chapters of Romans, Paul presented the gospel that is, "the power of God to salvation for everyone who believes, for the Jew first and also for the Greek" (1:16). In this chapter, Paul is going to examine the Jewish nation's past, present, and future relationship to God as seen in light of that gospel.

1. Paul appears to take a detour from this doctrinal teaching to talk about the role of the Israelites in God's plan. Based on what you have learned so far, how do you think this chapter fits into the larger context of Romans?

2. Paul was considered a traitor to Judaism by his fellow countrymen. Though his people had caused him great pain and hardship, he deeply loved them. What does Romans 9:3 reveal about the depth of Paul's love?

3. Though Israel has rejected the gospel, they are still holding their position in the Old Testament. List all the historical spiritual advantages of the Jewish people found in Romans 9:4.

4. Paul's heart was filled with great sorrow and continual grief because the Jews rejected Jesus as their Messiah. Like Paul, we should grieve and sorrow for the lost who reject God's offer of salvation through His Son, Jesus Christ. They will be eternally damned and separated from God. What do you learn about hell from the following verses?

    • Matthew 13:41-42, 49-50

    • Matthew 25:41

    • John 3:36

- Revelation 14:11

- Revelation 20:10-15

- Revelation 21:8

5. Why is it easy for us to become cynical about the unbelieving world?

6. How can we cultivate a heart of great sorrow and continual grief for the lost?

Day 2
Israel's Rejection and God's Purpose

Read Romans 9:6-13.

1. The failure of the Jews to respond to the gospel of Christ did not mean God's Word had failed. Do you believe that God's Word has failed you because you have not yet seen the salvation of friends and families you have prayed for? Why or why not?

2. "For they are not all Israel, who are of Israel (Romans 9:6)." In order to better understand what Paul is arguing here, consider the church today. We could say, "They are not all the Church, who are of the Church. Why would this be a true statement?

3. In Romans 9:7 and 10, Paul uses two examples from the Old Testament, to prove that God works on the principle of *election*, which mean that God chooses according to His own sovereign will and sets aside all human ideas of merit and superiority.

   • Which of Abraham's sons did God choose to establish His covenant with according to Genesis 17:21?

   • What did the Lord say to Rebekah concerning her older son Esau and her younger son Jacob in Genesis 25:23?

4. Romans 9:11 reveals a key truth, "(for the children not yet being born, nor having done any good or evil, that the purpose of God according to election might stand; not of works but of Him who calls). God's promises are based upon His own purposes, purposes He has already determined as One who lives outside of time. Read and note from Ephesians 1:4-11, God's own sovereign plans that have been determined before the world was created.

5. Write out 2 Peter 3:9 in its entirety. Take a moment to pray for friends and family who are lost and need Christ.

Day 3
Israel's Rejection and God's Justice

Read Romans 9:14-24.

1. To better comprehend what Paul is communicating in today's verses, we need to study Exodus 32. Write a short summary of the events that take place in Exodus 32.

2. Based on the events at Sinai, Paul makes his case to the Jew. "If you are going to say that God is unrighteous because He chooses one man and not another, then was God unrighteous at Sinai when He let you all live?" According to Exodus, 33:19 what truth does God speak to Moses? Write out the verse here.

3. Do you have a problem with God "being gracious to whom He will be gracious, and God having compassion on whom He will have compassion (Exodus 33:19)?" Why or why not?

4. God used the hard heart of Pharoah to demonstrate His power in order that His name would be declared in all the earth. There is a lot of confusion surrounding the *hardness* of Pharaoh's heart and God's involvement with his condition. Alva J. McClain provides an accurate illustration:

   Imagine a man goes to bed and sets an alarm clock. The first morning it goes off, he gets up. But after a week he says, "I will sleep a little longer." There will come a time when he will not even hear the clock go off. You say, that is a law of nature," but who is behind nature? In other words the God ordained psychological laws take their course, and it may be said that a man hardens himself, and yet in the ultimate sense God hardens him. And so, the man goes into a church and hears the gospel, and first of all rejects it, then keeps on hardening his heart, the heart will just go on hardening. God will finally step in and keep on hardening the man's heart. "[xlvii]

   Read the warning in Hebrews 3:12-14. What is a hard heart linked to in these verses and what are believers commanded to do in order to avoid this condition?

5. "What if God, willing to shew His wrath, and to make His power known, endured with much longsuffering the vessels of wrath fitted to destruction: And that He might make known the riches of His glory on the vessels of mercy, which he had afore prepared unto glory (Romans 9:22-23 KJV)." It's important that we clarify Paul's argument in these verses. Pastor John MacArthur clarifies:

    "Now I don't want to get too deep and I just want to give you one or two thoughts. Notice, there are vessels of wrath, at the end of verse 22, fitted to destruction. In verse 23, vessels of mercy which He had prepared to glory. Now in the Greek you have two serious distinctions here in the Greek tense and you must recognize them. I should say in the Greek voice which is similar to English. You realize the difference between active and passive? In active, the subject does the acting and in passive the subject receives the action. Now notice, verse 22 is a passive, vessels of wrath fitted to destruction. God is not the subject. The verb is passive. Verse 23, vessels of mercy which He had prepared to glory. God, there, is the subject and the verb is active.

    Listen, God says I prepare vessels for glory, but vessels are prepared for destruction. And what is happening there in the Greek tense, is God is taking one step away from the responsibility of preparing a person from His creative act for hell. God doesn't take that responsibility. He says there are vessels that have been prepared for destruction. And if you study the Bible very carefully you will see that everywhere in Scripture the responsibility for such preparation lies right in the very heart of the man who goes to hell. Is that right? Jesus said, "You will not come to me, that you might have life." At the end of the Book of Revelation He says, "Come, and let him that is thirsty come." And so God says, I fit for glory, but vessels are fitted for destruction. Judas was not created by God to occupy hell. Judas was not created by God to occupy hell.

    Another reason I know that is that hell was never even made for human beings. It was made for the devil and his angels. Judas went there because Judas chose to betray Christ, chose to reject the truth, and chose to pay a sad, sad price."[xlviii]

    How do people prepare themselves for destruction? Use Scripture to support your answer.

Day 4
Jesus Christ – The Stumbling Block

Read Romans 9:25-33.

1. According to Romans 9:30-32, how did the Gentiles pursuit of righteousness differ from that of the Jew?

2. Read Matthew 21:42-44. In one way or another, people will stumble or be offended by Jesus and His gospel. Why do you think people would rather be "ground to powder" than accept their need for Jesus?

3. Jesus said in Matthew 11:6, "Blessed is he who is not offended by Me." It is easy to accuse the unbelieving world of being offended by Jesus, but what about believers?

   • Are you offended when Jesus asks you to submit to your husband?
   • Are you offended when Jesus asks you to forgive your enemies?
   • Are you offended when Jesus asks you to die to your selfish desires?

   Share some circumstances in your own life where you wrestled with the convicting work of the Holy Spirit and the Word of God.

4. In Matthew 15:8-9, Jesus refers to the Pharisee's ignorant religious opposition as rooted in hearts that were far from God, and in teaching as truth man's own rules and views as if they were from God. Give some examples of the ways we honor God with our lips knowing that our hearts are far from Him.

Day 5
Reflection

1. Does God's right to choose relieve man of responsibility? Why or why not?

2. *"It is a solemn possibility to be a member of the visible church and not a member of the invisible church. It is possible to be humanly numbered among the people of God and yet not be a true child of God. It is also important to note that spiritual life does not come through physical birth. Your father and your mother, and all your family as far back as you can trace, may be Christians, but that won't make you a Christian any more that it made Ishmael and Esau Israelites because they were born of Abraham and Isaac."*[xlix]

   Take a moment to heed Paul's instruction in 2 Corinthians 13:5, "Examine yourselves as to whether you are in the faith. Test yourselves. Do you not know yourselves, that Jesus Christ is in you?—unless indeed you are disqualified." Are you merely professing Christ or do you possess Christ? Explain your answer.

3. "What an amazing thing God is doing in our world as He weaves our choices, good or bad, into a plan that He has destined to ultimately cause all things to glorify Him. Our only real decision is whether we want to be a vessel of honor or a vessel of dishonor. Israel has temporarily been set aside to dishonor because of their hard hearts. May our hearts be soft and may we become true children of faith and promise as God's purposes move us through this fallen world."[l]

   2 Timothy 2:20-21 makes it very clear we play a central role in whether or not we become a vessel of honor or dishonor. What do these verses teach us?

LESSON 8
Romans 9:1 – 9:33

Notes

LESSON 9: BEAUTIFUL FEET
Bringing a Message of Peace
Romans 10:1-21

LESSON 9
Romans 10:1 – 10:21

BEAUTIFUL FEET
Bringing a Message of Peace

Paul was heading to Damascus with orders to persecute Jews who had become Christians. His anger and hatred toward Christians and what they believed was fierce. Jesus met Paul along the way. His misdirected wrath towards believers was exchanged for a new understanding of the righteous way of God. Afterward, Paul devoted his life toward spreading the gospel.

The message that Paul carried was a wonderful message of freedom. His Jewish brethren were zealous for God but their zeal set them up for failure. The New American Commentary states, "Although law points us in the right direction, it provides no power to achieve its demands. It was never meant as a way to merit God's favor. Its role was to reflect the character of God in terms of ethical goals. The Jewish legalists had perverted the divine intention of the law and made it into a way to gain God's favor based on personal merit."[li]

We are all familiar with the pursuit of favor based on personal merit. It is a familiar feature of our culture. A common aphorism is, *if you work hard you can achieve anything.* We know by experience that nothing worthwhile can be achieved without hard work. If we are being honest, we would include, the righteousness of God. We know that this is wrong and that in the end it brings condemnation. We even know that, "The only thing God requires of people is that they not persist in trying to earn what they can only receive as a totally free gift. Their problem is that pride stands in the way of receiving God's gift. Deeply ingrained in people's hostility to divine grace is a proud and stubborn self-reliance that would rather suffer loss than be deprived of an occasion for boasting."[lii]

The only cure for this deeply ingrained hostility is the gospel. This is why beautiful feet are needed to bring the message of peace. To proclaim to those who are held captive by the world and its fleshly pursuits that, "faith in Christ brings freedom!" Beautiful feet are needed to proclaim the salvation of God in our homes, in our neighborhoods, in our cities, throughout our country, and to the world. Will you proclaim His message?

"How beautiful upon the mountains are the feet of him who brings good news, who proclaims peace, who brings glad tidings of good things, who proclaims salvation, who says to Zion, "Your God reigns!" Your watchmen shall lift up their voices, with their voices they shall sing together; for they shall see eye to eye when the Lord brings back Zion. Break forth into joy, sing together, you waste places of Jerusalem! For the Lord has comforted His people, He has redeemed Jerusalem. The Lord has made bare His holy arm in the eyes of all the nations; and all the ends of the earth shall see the salvation of our God (Isaiah 52:7-10)."

MEMORY VERSE

"And how shall they preach unless they are sent? As it is written: "How beautiful are the feet of those how preach the gospel of peace, who bring glad tidings of good things."

Day 1
Israel Needs the Gospel

Read Romans 10:1-10:4.

Paul is clear to address the issue at hand – Israel needs the gospel; and so does the lost and hurting world we live in. Paul helps us to understand why Israel and the unbelieving world are at odds with God.

1. **They have a zeal for God, but not according to knowledge (Romans 10:2).**

   The Israelites were zealously religious. However, they erred in isolating sincerity and ceremony away from the truth as revealed in God's Word. Sincerity and ceremony are only parts of what makes a religion. The people attended services, flocked to the shrines, performed the rituals, and offered the sacrifices. But they did not worship according to knowledge or cultivate the righteousness of God.[liii]

   - Give some examples of the religious person in 2016. How are they zealous without knowledge?

   - What did Jesus teach the woman at the well in John 4:24?

   - What does it mean to worship God in spirit and in truth?

2. **They sought to establish their own righteousness (Romans 10:3).**

   There is an ignorance that comes from lack of opportunity, but Israel had many opportunities to be saved. In their case, it was an ignorance that stemmed from willful, stubborn resistance to the truth. They would not submit to God. They were proud of their own good works and religious self-righteousness and would not admit their sins and trust the Savior.[liv]

   ***Good* people often have hearts that seek after the praise and honor of man. What are some ways moral people today seek to be applauded by man?**

3. Consider the culture that we live in today, where innate goodness is continually promoted. Tom Hovestol, in his book, *Extreme Righteousness: Seeing Ourselves in the Pharisees,* accurately diagnoses the problem -

    "A national *self-esteem movement* rightly sees the goodness but overlooks the evil. How much more true to life the balance of dignity and depravity that the Bible affirms! A *victimization movement* searches for causes outside ourselves for the flaws in our character and behavior. How much healthier to take responsibility for our faults without denying the reality that others do evil things to us as well. A *self-love movement* contends that if we only love ourselves, we could overcome most of the demons within. The Bible however, simply assumes that we naturally love ourselves (Ephesians 5:28-29, 33), and calls us by God's enablement to love God and others, neither of which is natural. Finally, the ever present self-help movement shouts compellingly from every bookstore and magazine rack, "You can do it! Marshal the goodness within and work hard enough at it, and nothing is impossible." This movement ignores the intoxicating pull of depravity and the necessity of God's help."[lv]

    How does the lie that we are innately good play into the strategy of the enemy?

4. Why is "Christ the end of the law for righteousness to everyone who believes (Romans 10:4)?"

Day 2
Believing and Confessing

Read Romans 10:6-13.

1. What would you say is the general view in the world today about how a person can get to heaven?

2. Do all paths lead to God? Why or why not? Use Scripture to support your answer.

3. Describe your moment of conversion. What circumstances led to your salvation, and how was the gospel preached to you?

4. "The word is near in your mouth and your heart... (Romans 10:8)." The gospel is within reach of every man. All a person needs to do to attain righteousness is to respond in faith to the gospel as it is preached. Why do believers often complicate sharing the gospel?

5. According to Romans 10:10 what must one do to be saved?

6. Why is faith in our hearts more important than a verbal confession from our mouths? (Romans 10:10)?

Salvation is offered to everyone;
We must accept it by believing and confessing that Jesus is Lord of our life.

Day Three
Beautiful Feet

Read Romans 10:14-15.

1. How can a person come to believe in Christ if they don't know about Christ? According to the following verses, what responsibility does the believer have to share Christ?

   • Matthew 28:19-20

   • Mark 16:15

   • 2 Corinthians 5:18, 20.

2. Are you fulfilling your responsibility to share Christ and make disciples? Why or why not? If your answer is no, what are some practical steps you can take to start sharing your faith?

3. Why is the gospel a gospel of peace? Use Scripture to support your answer.

4. According to Ephesians 6:15, the believer in Christ is to "shod their feet with the preparation of the gospel of peace." The word preparation used in Ephesians 6:15 comes from the Greek word *hetoimasia*. Vine's Complete Expository Dictionary of Old and New Testament Words has the following to say about the use of the word hetoimasia in this context: "The Gospel itself is to be the firm footing of the believer, his walk being worthy of it and therefore a testimony in regard to it."[lvi]

   How effective will a believer be that is only talking the gospel, but not walking it out too?

5. The enemies of the Roman Empire would sometimes place sharp, spiked objects on the ground in front of the soldiers before a battle. Any attacking soldier not wearing shoes substantial enough for the attack would soon find himself crippled or killed. Though the shoes were not by any means the most well-known part of the soldier's armor, they were vital. The same is true where the armor of God is concerned.

   Why is it important for believers to be aware of the spiritual battle they face when seeking to share the gospel?

Day 4
Israel Knows the Truth

Read Romans 10:16-21.

1. What is the heart of God concerning those who reject Him? Is it ever too late to return to God? Use Scripture to support your answer.

2. "Faith comes by hearing and hearing by the Word of God (Romans 10:17)." Israel heard the truth of the gospel, but they had not obeyed it (Romans 10:16). Paul refreshes their memory by quoting Moses and Isaiah. Once we know the truth, God holds us accountable to it. Why is this important to remember as we seek to live for Christ? Use Scripture to support your answer.

3. Knowledge of the Bible is useless unless it is applied. Share some ways that you have failed to live according to what you knew to be true.

4. In Romans 10:20-21, Paul quotes Isaiah 65:1-5. The verses listed below are from the New Living Translation.

   "The Lord says, "I was ready to respond, but no one asked for help. I was ready to be found, but no one was looking for me. I said, 'Here I am, here I am!' to a nation that did not call on my name. All day long I opened my arms to a rebellious people. But they follow their own evil paths and their own crooked schemes. All day long they insult me to my face by worshiping idols in their sacred gardens. They burn incense on pagan altars. At night they go out among the graves, worshiping the dead. They eat the flesh of pigs and make stews with other forbidden foods. Yet they say to each other, 'Don't come too close or you will defile me! I am holier than you! 'These people are a stench in my nostrils, an acrid smell that never goes away."

   What do you learn about God from these verses, and what do you learn about the hearts of Israel?

Day 5
Reflection

1. We read in our introduction that Romans 10:15 is not concerned with the external beauty of our feet, but the beauty of the message that we bear. Those with beautiful feet are those who preach the gospel of peace and bring the good news of Jesus Christ! How has the gospel brought peace into your life?

2. The Greek word *hōraios,* translated *beautiful*, can also be rendered *timely*, which means belonging to the right hour or season. This word conveys the sense of arriving at just the right time. In other words, "How timely are the feet (that is the arrival of) those proclaiming the good news!" Your feet are beautiful because they are designed to bring a timely message of peace to a world that is in pieces. Where do you feel called to go with the gospel?

3. Now that we know that God wants to use our beautiful feet, the question becomes are they willing to go? Doubt, fear, and insecurities keep our feet from walking into the darkness to bring the light of the gospel message. Be honest to evaluate your willingness to share the gospel. Face your doubts and fears by listing those things which may be holding you back from a passion to share Christ with the world.

4. Take each one of those struggles you listed above and find a Scripture you can use to hide in your heart. Use these verses as your weapon to overcome!

The World's Bible (Annie Johnson Flint)

Christ has no hands but our hands to do His work today;
He has no feet but our feet to lead men in His way;
He has no tongue but our tongues to tell men how He died;
He has no help but our help to bring them to His side.

We are the only Bible the careless world will read;
We are the sinner's gospel, we are the scoffer's creed;
We are the Lord's last message, given in deed and word;
What if the type is crooked? What if the print is blurred?

What if our hands are busy with other work than His?
What if our feet are walking where sin's allurement is?
What if our tongues are speaking of things His lips would spurn"
How can we hope to help Him and hasten His return?

LESSON 9
Romans 10:1 – 10:21

Notes

LESSON 10: PROMISES THAT NEVER FAIL
The Faithfulness of God
Romans 11:1-36

LESSON 10
Romans 11:1-36

Promises That Never Fail
The Faithfulness of God

The Jews were zealous for God, but they sought a relationship with Him on the basis of their own righteousness rather than His. The people of Israel had been blessed by God in many ways, including receiving His law, but they made the mistake of worshipping the law rather than allowing it to serve its intended purpose of leading them to Jesus. Because of their hard-heartedness and unwillingness to humble themselves and receive God's gift of grace, the Jews were rejected by God. But Israel's rejection of Jesus paved the way for God to open salvation up to the Gentiles.

The great news we receive this week, is despite Israel's unfaithfulness to God, all of Israel will be saved (Romans 11:26). If God broke His promises to Israel, you and I would have no hope. God keeps His promises! That truth this week should cause you to rejoice. He is not fickle, like we are and He doesn't change His mind. Scripture uses a big word for this unchanging character of God. It is called *immutability*. Numbers 23:19 teaches us that "God is not a man, so he does not lie. He is not human, so he does not change his mind. Has he ever spoken and failed to act? Has he ever promised and not carried it through?" Hebrews 6:18 adds that we can flee to Him for refuge with great confidence and hope because it is impossible for Him to lie. "So God has given both his promise and his oath. These two things are unchangeable because it is impossible for God to lie. Therefore, we who have fled to him for refuge can have great confidence as we hold to the hope that lies before us."

A. W. Tozer comments, "Is it not a wondrous strength to know that God changes not? That His attitude toward us now is the same as it was in eternity past and will be in eternity to come? What peace it brings to the Christian's heart to realize that our Heavenly Father never differs from Himself. In coming to Him at any time we need not wonder whether we shall find Him in a receptive mood. He is always receptive to misery and need, as well as to love and faith. He does not keep office hours nor set aside periods when He will see no one. Neither does He change His mind about anything. Today, this moment, He feels toward His creatures, toward babies, toward the sick, the fallen, the sinful, exactly as He did when He sent His only-begotten Son into the world to die for mankind."[lvii]

We serve an awesome and all-powerful God who is true to His promises and true to His Word. A relationship with Him serves as a strong foundation for our lives on which we can have a peace and joy that nothing else can offer. Through His mercy and grace we can have forgiveness and salvation from our sins. Our gracious God holds out His hands to us, and it is our responsibility to respond in submission and worship.[lviii]

MEMORY VERSE

Oh, the depth of the riches both of the wisdom and knowledge of God! How unsearchable are His judgments and His ways past finding out (Romans 11:33)!

Day 1
The Remnant of Israel

Read Romans 11:1-10.

The Old Testament scriptures are abounding with promises which God made to Israel concerning her land, her King, and her future salvation. Many of these promises are unconditional. For God to leave off working with Israel would require that scores and scores of biblical prophecies would go completely unfulfilled. Well then, what is happening with Israel? We must understand that there are two groups of Israelites. There is a small, believing remnant and there is a large remaining group of Israelites whose eyes are blinded to the truth.[lix]

1. Paul is addressing the Jews, using an Old Testament reference in Romans 11:2-4 to make a point. Study 1 Kings 19:11-18. What do these verses teach you about the faithfulness of God? How did Paul use the example of Elijah to encourage Israel?

2. Elijah lived during a dark period in the history of Israel (the northern kingdom). The king, Ahab, and his wicked, pagan wife Jezebel were leading the people away from the true worship of Jehovah to the false worship of Baal (the Canaanite fertility god). It was a time of great apostasy for the Israelites in general. Elijah felt that he was standing all alone. He felt that he was the only one left who was still honoring Jehovah, the true God. Everyone seemed to be a Baal worshipper except for himself. But Elijah was mistaken and God had to correct him.

    It is easy to feel alone in our Christianity when we see many Christians today living for the world. How do Paul's words to Elijah encourage you?

3. In Romans 11:1-4, Paul is describing the biblical concept of *remnant*. A remnant is a left-over amount from a larger portion or piece, whether it is food, material from which a garment is fashioned, or even a group of people. Although remnants could be looked upon as worthless scraps, and many times are, God assigned high value to those of His people whom He had set aside for holy purposes, those He labels as "remnants" in several places in the Bible.

    According to 2 Timothy 2:19, what assurance can God's remnant hold onto?

4. Would people know by the life that you live, that you are a part of God's faithful remnant? Explain your answer.

5. In Romans 11:5-8 identify the cause of the faith of *believing* Jews and identify the cause of the hardness of heart of *unbelieving* Jews?

Day 2
Salvation Has Come to the Gentiles

Read Romans 11:11-24.

1. According to Romans 11:11-12, how have Gentiles been helped by the Jews' rejection of God's salvation plan?

2. Looking at Romans 11:13-14, how did Paul hope his own Jewish people would respond when they saw him ministering to the Gentiles?

3. In what ways can a believer live a life that will cause people to be "jealous" of her salvation?

4. Paul addresses his Gentile Christian readers to warn them against pride (Romans 11:18), haughtiness (Romans 11:20), and complacency (Romans 11:22). Explain how these three characteristics can cause us to end up like the Jews with blind, hardened hearts.

5. Read Romans 11:16-24. Using the outline of the tree below illustrate what Paul is describing in these verses. Take some time to be creative with colors, markers and additional symbols.

Day 3
A Future Reception

Read Romans 11:25-32.

Today is a good time to review what we have been learning about Israel in Romans 9-11. Paul has been addressing one primary question: Did God's promise fail since Israel largely rejected Jesus as the Messiah? Up until today's reading Paul has provided six different answers.

- A true Israelite is anyone who has the faith of Abraham, not just those who are born Jews (9:6-24).
- God always said that not all Israel would be saved and that some Gentiles would be (9:25-29).
- The unbelief of the Jews was their own responsibility, not God's (9:30-10:21).
- Some Jews (Paul included) have believed and been saved (11:1). God has always worked through a remnant (11:2-10).
- The salvation of the Gentiles is meant to arouse Israel to jealousy and be the means of saving some of them (11:11-24).

Our text today gives us the seventh answer: in the end all Israel will be saved, and everyone will see that God has honored His promise toward Israel on a national basis. (Romans 11:25-32).

1. Paul explains in Romans 11:25, that Israel's salvation is a mystery of God. According to this verse, how had Israel responded to the message Paul preached? When would Israel's period of hardness end?

2. What promise has God made to Israel in Romans 11:26-27?

3. Explain the two contrasting ways the Jews are described in Romans 11:28. Then, using Ephesians 2:1-10, describe your own personal testimony.

4. Why is Romans 11:29 a comforting assurance?

106

5. We learn a tremendous truth about God from the way He deals with Israel. God chose the nation of Israel as His own, and He remains faithful to His choice even after their rejection of God. What additional insights do you gain about this attribute of God from Hebrews 6:18 and James 1:17?

Day 4
Paul's Praise

Read Romans 11:33-36.

At the beginning of chapter 9, Paul was filled with great sorrow and grief for his unsaved countrymen. But as he has laid out God's incredible plan of salvation for both the Gentile and the Jew, all he can do is praise God!

1. What is the answer to all of Paul's three questions in Romans 11:34?

2. It is not a surprise that Paul's contemplation of the divine attributes of God leads him to the worship and adoration of God. List at least 5 or 6 of God's attributes that you would be interested in studying.

3. When is the last time you considered the awesomeness of God? What brought about the moment?

4. Romans 11:33-36 is described as a *doxology*. The dictionary defines *doxology* as a *hymn or form of words containing an ascription of praise to God.* Write out Paul's doxology from 1 Timothy 6:15-16.

5. Using 3 or 4 sentences, write out your own expression of praise to God

Day 5
Reflection

1. Given what you have studied about Israel, how do current events in Israel speak to Bible prophecy? Why is it important for believers to pray and support Israel?

2. There are no hopeless cases when it comes to God. How does the truth of Israel's future fill you with hope for the salvation of those you are praying for?

3. If God had not been merciful to you while you went your own way and did your own thing, describe where your life might be now.

4. Review all of chapter 11 and select 2 verses that are an encouragement to you. Write them out in their entirety and explain why you chose them.

LESSON 10
Romans 11:1-36

Notes

LESSON 11: A ROMANS 12 CHRISTIAN
Living in Light of the Gospel
Romans 12:1-13:14

LESSON 11
Romans 12:1-13:14

A Romans 12 Christian
Living in Light of the Gospel

Romans 12:1 is fitting for our focus this week, "I beseech you therefore, brethren, by the mercies of God, that you present your bodies a living sacrifice, holy, acceptable to God, which is your reasonable service." What is the *therefore*, therefore? Paul is pleading with you and me to consider all the glorious truths of the gospel that we have learned up until this point. In light of what we have been given in Christ, how can our response be anything less than a sacrifice of our entire lives to Him?

Paul taught us in the first chapter of Romans that transformed lives begin with the gospel message of Christ, for *in it is the power of God*. It is the gospel that brings us salvation: "For I am not ashamed of the gospel of Christ, for it is the power of God to salvation for everyone who believes, for the Jew first and also for the Greek. For in it the righteousness of God is revealed from faith to faith; as it is written, "The just shall live by faith (Romans 1:16-17).""

Transformation or Christ-like change can be defined as the process of growth toward wholeness in Christ. It is the journey of being transformed by the Holy Spirit and God's Word into the likeness of Christ. "The ultimate goal of Christianity is *transformation*. Believers in Christ are to change from unrighteous to righteous, from takers to givers, from hearers to doers, from people of the world to people of God, from self-centered to Christ-centered, from lovers of the flesh to lovers of the Spirit, from independent to interdependent, from inevitable death to everlasting life."[lx] In a sentence, transformation in the Christian life is a dramatic shift from living a life that conforms to the ways of the world, to living a life that pleases God. This change takes place through the renewing of the believer's mind. The renewing of the believer's mind creates an inward change of heart that manifests itself in outward actions. Evidence of transformation is seen in a believer's life as they continue to grow and increasingly reflect Christ and glorify Him in their everyday living.

In Ephesians 4:22-24, Paul teaches us to "put off our former conduct, the old woman which grows corrupt according to her deceitful lusts, and be renewed in the spirit of her mind, in order to put on the new woman which was created according to God, in true righteousness and holiness." Don't forget what Paul taught in Roman's chapter 8, that this new life is led by the Spirit of God (Romans 8:13-14).

Without change or transformation in our lives, our testimonies are powerless to impact the unbelieving world around us.

MEMORY VERSE

"And do not be conformed to this world, but be transformed by the renewing of your mind so that you may prove what is that good and acceptable and perfect will of God (Romans 12:2)."

Day 1
Living Sacrifices

Read Romans 12:1-8.

Romans 12 begins with a critical and important "therefore." Paul is beseeching or "pleading" with the Roman believers to live out what they have learned in the previous eleven chapters. How could our response to God's mercy be anything less than total surrender?

1. Romans 12:1-3 contains four commands that are key to the Christian life. Take each one of the four and explain their function in the life of the believer.

   - Be Consecrated (Romans 12:1).

   - Don't be Conformed (Romans 12:2).

   - Be Transformed (Romans 12:2).

   - Maintain a Proper Self Perspective (Romans 12:3).

2. A believer in Christ is to have an accurate view of themselves. What are the dangers of a self-perspective that is too high or too low? Is your view of yourself too high or too low? Explain.

3. Before Paul teaches on the spiritual gifts, he teaches about the church, the Body of Christ in Romans 12:4-5. Study the two parallel passages in 1 Corinthians 12:4-27 and Ephesians 4:11-16. Summarize what you learned about the importance of your place in the Body of Christ.

4. In Romans 12:6-8, seven gifts are listed. These gifts are commonly known as the motivational gifts which form our life and service to God. Identify the gifts in the chart below and explain how each gift is to be used. Also place a checkmark beside the gift you believe best describes your personal gifting.

Spiritual Gifts	How to Use Them

5. In the Old Testament, not just any animal could be used in sacrifice; it had to be the best or it would not be an acceptable offering. Are you giving God the best of your time, talents and resources? Why or why not?

Day 2
Serving in Love

Read Romans 12:9-21.

1. "Let love be without hypocrisy (Romans 12:9a)." In Greek drama, actors held large masks over their faces to represent the character they were portraying. The hypocrite is a person who masks her real self while playing a part for those around her. Christ is calling us to be open, honest and above board with one another. Our lives should be like an open book, easily read. At the heart of true community is honesty.

   Do you find it difficult to be yourself around other believers, why or why not?

2. "Abhor evil, cling to what is good (Romans 12:9b)." Genuine love isn't just based on our emotions. The two commandments that are presented together with the command to love one another demonstrate that true love ought to be united with hating what is evil and clinging to what is good. This kind of love is based on the truth. It's a love which seeks what's best for the people we love. It doesn't try to hide reality in order to please the other person; it pursues that which is best in the long run, even when it may hurt for a little while.

   Give a few examples of circumstances where believers are to speak the truth to one another in love. Why is this such a difficult command to obey?

3. Romans 12:9-13 describes the way in which we are to serve one another in love as Christ loves us. Christ-like love chooses to give another person what they need most, when they deserve the least and at great personal cost. Read Luke 10:30-37. What good excuses do you suppose the priest and the Levite had for passing on the other side of the road and not stopping to help? What are some of the excuses we use for not stopping and helping those around us who are in need?

4. The word *supernatural* is defined as; *of or relating to the immediate exercise of divine power; miraculous.* We need to know right from the beginning that without the supernatural power of God, the commands found in Romans 12:14-21 are impossible to keep. When we have been hurt, or an injustice has taken place, our natural response is to *fight back*, *get back* and *pay back*. Yet, God calls us to a higher standard. If we are to embrace Christ's teaching, it will be the most difficult, demanding, and uncomfortable thing we have ever been asked to do.

How do we see Jesus in Luke 23:32-37 model the way we are to respond to the evil aimed at us?

5. "Do not be overcome by evil, but overcome evil with good." In his book, *How to Overcome Evil*, Jay E. Adams writes, "Good is the most powerful, most aggressive, most violent force one could possibly use. God is creative at helping us come up with ways we can show good to those who hate us. While our ultimate goal is to win over the opposing party into a good relationship with God and with us, this method provides a remarkable side benefit. Plotting and executing a strategy of kindness shifts our focus from a brittle, eroding defense to a creative, energized offense. And before you say, "This will never work," remember, "Love never fails."[lxi]

Give some practical examples of way believers can overcome evil with good.

Day 3
Submit to Authority

Romans 13:1-7.

Christianity and good citizenship go together.

1. Where do earthly governmental authorities get their ultimate authority to rule?

2. Submitting to government authority goes much further than simply obeying laws. What additional insights do you discover from 1 Timothy 2:1-3 and 1 Peter 2:13-17?

3. Although believers are to submit to government authority, they are not commanded to support laws that stand in opposition to the Word of God. What are some laws of the government which directly oppose the Word of God?

4. Where does the authority of government end and the authority of God begin? Use Acts 5:26-32 and any other Scriptures that come to mind to help support your answer.

Day 4
Put on Christ

Read Romans 13:8-14.

1. What does Paul mean when he teaches "that love is fulfillment of the law (Romans 13:8)?"

2. Read 1 Corinthians 13:4-8a. List the characteristics of love.

3. Using the chart below evaluate your current relationships to see if you are loving according to the characteristics you listed above.

   Rate yourself accordingly:

   HIGH (obedient to 1 Corinthians 13:4-8a).
   MEDIUM (sometimes obedient to 1 Corinthians 13:4-8a).
   LOW (usually disobedient to 1 Corinthians 13:4-8a).
   MISSING IN ACTION (not interested in obeying at all 1 Corinthians 13:4-8a)

MY RELATIONSHPS	MY LEVEL OF LOVING
Spouse	
Children	
Mother	
Father	
Friends	
Coworkers	
Church Family	
Neighbors	
Strangers	

4. How can you grow in love for those who are in your sphere of influence?

5. Romans 13:11-14 is nicknamed the believer's wakeup call! What should we be taking off in our lives and what should we be putting on?

Day 5
Reflection

1. Romans 12:2 in the J.B. Philipps translation reads, "Don't let the world around you squeeze you into its own mold, but let God re-mold your minds from within, so that you may prove in practice that the plan of God for you is good, meets all His demands and moves towards the goal of true maturity. How does the world try to squeeze you into its mold?

2. Reflect on the life you are living. Share any evidence you have that you are becoming more transformed by Christ than becoming conformed to the world.

3. What do you believe is the greatest obstacle to your serving God more faithfully with your gifts?

4. Paul sounds the alarm at the end of chapter 13. What does he mean when he says that our "salvation is nearer than when we first believed (Romans 13:11)?" Why is the wisdom Paul provides in Romans 13:12-14 vital as we seek to be victorious in these last days?

LESSON 11
Romans 12:1-13:14

Notes

LESSON 12: LOVE OR LIBERTY
That is the Question
Romans 14:1-16:27

LESSON 12
Romans 14:1-16:27

Love or Liberty
That is the Question

Christian liberty is the freedom a believer enjoys as it relates to things that are not forbidden in the Bible. In Christianity, these things are referred to as *adiaphora.* "Adiaphora was the ancient term for theological beliefs that, while important, were not central to the Christian faith."[lxii] These liberties might include drinking alcohol, gambling, smoking, Halloween, dancing, listening to secular music, attending R-rated movies, and even whether you can be a Republican or a Democrat! These are topics that the Bible is silent on, yet believers are commanded to use their liberty wisely. God is not silent on how we are to handle these matters in order to keep believers from arguing and dividing over them. It is not uncommon to hear a believer say, "I am free to do anything I want." Get any group of believers together to discuss their liberties and you are certain to find an emotionally charged discussion! Though Christians have many things they agree upon, it's appalling to see what they can fight about! It is not uncommon to find churches that have split over these issues, nor is it unusual to see a friendship lost as a result.

It is true that Christ died and rose again to set us free. He fulfilled the law (Matthew 5:17). But our liberty must be kept in proportion to our love. Paul teaches in 1 Corinthians 10:23 that "all things are lawful." Paul does not stop there. Even though all things are lawful, he asks his readers to pause and question, are all things *helpful* and do they *edify*? Where Scripture is silent on many matters, believers in Christ have the freedom to make their own decisions. Unfortunately, many in the church today, make these judgments hastily, without considering the implications of their choices.

In Romans 14:1-15:13, Paul describes two groups of people who are at odds with each other over two areas of concern. We have wisdom to gain from the examples that he presents. It is important as we study through these chapters together, to keep an open mind and be willing to lay aside our differences. We want to hear what the Spirit has to say to us. If we are teachable, our relationships with others will be more Christ-like and God will get all the glory.

Unity in the body of Christ was a top priority for Paul. He was a man who walked the talk and enjoyed healthy, vibrant, and deep friendships with his fellow believers. As we end our study, we have the opportunity to meet many of Paul's friends, who supported him in the work of the ministry. His parting words to the Roman readers then and to us today are priceless.

MEMORY VERSE

"Receive one who is weak in the faith, but not to disputes over doubtful things (Romans 14:1)."

Day 1

Weak in the Faith

Read Romans 14:1-23.

It is important that we accurately define the one who is weak according to Romans chapter 14. Alva J. McClain comments: "What does "weak in the faith" mean? Those who are weak in the faith are Christians who have not laid hold by faith upon these wonderful things that have been unfolded in the book of Romans. They are people who have not yet been able to apprehend and grasp full and free salvation as it is revealed in the Lord Jesus Christ. They have not grasped entirely that wonderful proposition in Romans 8:1 which says that in the Son of God there can be no condemnation whatever! They have not grasped the fact that salvation is apart from all works and the Christian, when she enters into Christ, leaves legalism and ceremonialism and all other "isms" behind her and is free."[lxiii]

1. It is likely that the weak believers Paul is speaking about are Jewish Christians. If that is the case, why is it understandable they would be weak in the faith?

2. According to Romans 14:1, what is our attitude to be towards those who are "weak in the faith?"

3. Paul identifies two non-moral issues, food and the observance of special days. Cite some way believers divide over these two issues today.

4. What are some other liberties that cause division among believers today?

5. The two groups mentioned in this chapter are the weak and the strong. Which of these two groups is right? Explain your answer. Why do both groups need correction?

6. Don't miss what Paul is teaching in Romans 14:13, 15, 20 and 21.

- Why do you think Paul addresses the weaker person by telling him not to judge (13)?

- Why do you think Paul addresses the stronger person by telling him not to grieve (15)?

- Why does Paul tell both groups not to destroy the work of God (20)?

- What is Paul's final command to the strong (21)?

Day 2
Glorify God Together

Read Romans 15:1-13.

1. How are strong and weak believers to treat one another according to Romans 15:5-7?

2. Unity means like-mindedness. Does this mean that Christians have to do the same things in everything? Why or why not? Use Scripture to support your answer.

3. Is there any issue you are holding onto which has prevented you from joining with others to glorify God with one heart and one mouth (Romans 15:6)?

4. In what way does a deep desire to, glorify the God and Father of our Lord Jesus Christ," push out the attitude of wanting to assert your rightness and opinions, or engage in disputes over nonessential matters?

5. The Messianic king was to be of the family of Jesse the father of David. In Romans 15:12 Paul is quoting Isaiah 11:10. Jesus is a branch or descendant of the family of Jesse, as well as of David. Paul concludes with a reminder to the Gentiles to look to Christ, for that is where their true hope could be found. Explain what it means to abound in hope by the power of the Holy Spirit (Romans 15:13).

Day 3
Ministers of Christ Jesus

Read Romans 15:14-33.

1. Carefully read today's text. Paul was a church planter. Describe the heart of a missionary and church planter from the passage you are studying today.

2. Paul was confident of three characteristics that the Roman believers shared (Romans 15:14). Explain why each character trait is important in the life of the believer. Use Scripture to support your answer.

   - Full of Goodness

   - Filled with all knowledge

   - Able to admonish one another

3. Why should you feel confident, through the grace of God, in your ability to be a minister of Jesus Christ (Romans 15:16)?

4. Who has been "a Paul" in your life? How has that person given you hope and courage, and how has she helped you grow spiritually?

5. To whom can you be "a Paul"? How do you think you can help her grow spiritually?

6. Paul knew the value of prayer. We all need the prayers of the saints to cover us as we seek to fulfill our God-given missions. Look up and cite 3 verses on prayer in their entirety that speak to the importance of prayer in a believer's life.

Day 4
Parting Words

Read Romans 16:1-27.

1. Write a brief introduction of yourself to a church in another country. Explain your purpose and mission. How will you give glory to God for what He has done in your life?

2. What do you learn about Paul's friends who served alongside him in ministry? In what ways do their examples inspire you?

    *   Phoebe

    *   Priscilla and Aquila

    *   Mary

    *   Andronicus and Junia

    *   Tryphena and Tryphosa

    *   Persis

3. Before Paul closes his letter to the Romans, he gives them one last warning about "those who cause divisions and offenses, contrary to the doctrine which you have learned... (Romans 16:17)." Why do you think Paul instructs believers to avoid these people? Use Scripture to support your answer.

4. Paul closes with a beautiful benediction in Romans 16:25-27. "The gospel is neither human in its origin nor its power. The gospel is the truth of God's love for all mankind. It is communicated to us through the power of His Word, revealed by His Spirit. Its origins are in God. It is accomplished by God, and has God's own glory as its goal. It is, as Paul says, a "mystery kept secret before the world since the world began for long ages past, but now made manifest, and by the prophetic Scriptures made known to all nations, according to the commandment of the everlasting God, for obedience to the faith."[lxiv]

Why is nothing in the world greater than Jesus and His gospel?

Let's join with Paul and declare,
"To God, alone, wise, be glory through Jesus Christ forever. Amen (Romans 15:27)."

Day 5
Reflection

1. Read Galatians 5:1 and Galatians 5:13. What have you learned about your Christian liberties as a result of these verses and this week's study? Explain how you can both protect your freedom in Christ, yet also willingly limit it.

2. When it comes to the gray areas of Scripture where the Bible is silent, a believer is free to choose. How can you use the following Scriptures to help you make wise choices regarding your Christian liberties?

   - Romans 14:17

   - Romans 14:19

   - Romans 15:1-3

   - 1 Corinthians 6:12

   - 1 Corinthians 8:13

3. Imagine how the Gentiles and Jewish believers responded to Paul's letter. Describe what they might have concluded as they finished reading his letter.

4. Summarize in a paragraph or two your response to Paul's letter. How has the Book of Romans impacted your life? What was your favorite lesson and how will you act upon what you have learned?

GLOSSARY
TOP 20 ROMAN TERMS

These definitions are not exhaustive. They were selected to help provide a basic understanding of the theological themes covered in the book of Romans. Definitions are provided by Holman.

1. **Accountability** – Subject to giving an account, answerable, a statement explaining one's conduct. Every believer in Christ will give an account of himself to God. Also, as members of the Body of Christ God calls us to accountability with one another for the purpose of encouragement, protection, exhortation and correction. *See Romans 14:12.*

2. **Adoption** – Most people would rather have been born into a loving family than adopted into one. But with respect to God's family, both—birth and adoption—happen to believers at once. Anyone who believes in Jesus is born of God and is also adopted by God into His family. The Greek word for "adoption" comes from two words put together: *huios*, meaning "son," and *thesis*, meaning "a placing." Thus, the word means "placement into sonship." The Greek word is a legal term that indicates that believers have been given all the legal privileges of being sons in God's family. When God adopts believers as His children, He places the Spirit of His Son into their hearts so that they become, in effect, His natural-born children. As such, they are not merely "adopted" (in the sense the word now conveys) but genuinely "begotten" by God. God makes "sons of God" out of "sons of men." The term "sons of God," a common King James expression, includes believers of both sexes. *See Romans 8:15, 23, and 9:4.*

3. **Circumcision** - The ritual practice of removing the foreskin of an individual, which was commanded for all male Israelites in OT times as a sign of participation in the covenant God established with Abraham (Genesis 17: 9– 14). The teaching of the New Testament affirms that a faithful believer, though physically uncircumcised, is regarded by God as spiritually circumcised (Romans 2:25–29). Both Jews and Gentiles are saved by grace and circumcised and uncircumcised alike are justified on the ground of their faith, apart from obeying the law (Rom 3:28–30). People of the Old Testament were reminded of God's covenant through circumcision. Christians today have the knowledge of the Holy Spirit as well as the Bible to remind us that God's love for us is eternal. *See Romans 2:25-29, 3:1, 4:9, 4:11-12, and 15:8.*

4. **Condemnation** – To be pronounced guilty or deserving punishment. By nature, every human is born into sin, guilty of transgression and deserving God's punishment. Jesus Christ took upon Himself the sin of the world and carried each man's guilt to the cross thus pronouncing all believers innocent and justified. *See Romans 3:18, 5:16, 5:18, and 8:1.*

5. **Edification or Edify** – The act of building a structure. To instruct, improve or build up spiritually. Jesus Christ came to earth to bring man into a relationship with His Father. He calls all believers to live and behave in such a way as to building up and encouraging one another spiritually. *See Romans 14:19 and 15:2.*

6. **Faith** - Faith is one of those words that Christians use often. Even so, it is one of the most difficult words to define. Just what is faith? The writer of Hebrews wrote, "Now faith is the assurance of things hoped for, the conviction of things not seen" (Hebrews 11:1 NLT). Faith is belief in Jesus Christ as the Son of God who saves. It is by faith that believers are justified, reconciled, redeemed, made alive, adopted into the family of God. (Romans 8:15–16), recreated, and set free. James speaks of faith as being perfected by works. He rejected the concept of faith without resulting action—that is, believing something is true without founding one's life on it and acting upon it. Faith apart from works is not real faith. It is barren and, thus, not genuine faith at all. In Paul's letters, he writes about faith from a number of angles. He sets faith over and against works of the law as the only and true basis for being made right with God (Romans 1- 4) and appeals to Abraham to prove his point: "Abraham believed God, and it was reckoned to him as righteousness" (Romans 4:3). Salvation is entirely apart from the law (Romans 3:21)—righteousness is the gift of God through faith in Christ. *See Romans 1:5, 1:8, 1:12, 1:16-17, 3:3, 3:21-22, 3:25-31, 4:1, 4:5, 4:9, 4:11, 4:12-14, 4:16, 4:19, 4:20, 5:1-5:2, 9:30, 9:32, 10:6, 10:8, 10:17, 11:20, 12:3, 12:6, 14:1, 14:22-23, 16:26.*

7. **Flesh and Spirit-** Terms noticeably used in tandem in the New Testament to contrast diametrically opposed lifestyles. The term "flesh" is often ascribed the connotation of an ungodly lifestyle of selfishness and sensual self-gratification. The term "Spirit" signifies the opposite characteristics. One who walks by the Spirit lives with a conspicuous God consciousness that directs his or her dispositions, attitudes, and actions. This use of these terms is evident especially in Paul's writing. In Romans 7 Paul spoke frankly about his constant struggle between the continuing power of his flesh and the sincere intentions of his will to live obediently to God. Even though believers wrestle with the flesh, those who are in Jesus Christ are no longer under compulsion to live in a fleshly manner. In Galatians 5 Paul provides the most extensive treatment of this subject. He encourages Christians who indeed "live by the Spirit" also to "walk by the Spirit" so that they may avoid carrying "out the desire of the flesh." The admonition here as well as in other Pauline passages is for Christians not to live carnally. A carnal Christian is a believer who, although regenerate, persists in living a life ruled by fleshly desires. *"Flesh" See Romans 1:3, 2:28, 3:20, 4:1, 6:19 7:5, 7:18, 7:25, 8:1, 8:3-5, 8:8-9, 8:12-13, 9:3, 9:5, 9:8, 11:14, 13;14.*
"Spirit" See Romans 1:4, 1:9, 1:11, 2:29, 5:5, 7:6, 7:14, 8:1-2, 8:4-5, 8:6, 8:9-16, 8:23, 8:26-27, 9:1-11:8.

8. **Gospel** - The Christian gospel is the good news of God's salvation for man provided through Christ's substitutionary death and bodily resurrection. The gospel of salvation originates in God's sovereign grace and is experienced only through personal faith in Jesus Christ. The gospel was the center of Paul's preaching and the rule by which he conducted himself to the glory of God. Paul employs *euangelion* 60 of the 75 times it is used in the NT. The congregations he addressed knew the content of the gospel, seen by the fact that Paul used the term without qualification 28 times. He also qualifies the term: the "gospel of Christ" (9 times), "the gospel of God" (6 times), "the gospel of peace," "the gospel of our salvation," and so forth. When Paul uses *euangelizomai*, it carries the same meaning as *kerusso*, both describing the act of preaching the gospel.

In 1 Corinthians 15 and Romans 1, Paul explains the content of the gospel he preached. *See Romans 1:1, 1:9, 1:15-16, 2:16, 10:1, 10:14-16, 11:28, 15:16, 15:19-20, 15:29, 16:25.*

9. **Grace** –The term grace or favor is used in Scripture generally to indicate God's free and unmerited favor toward men, particularly His redeemed people. God's grace includes both His attitude and action of love, mercy, and kindness for undeserving people. The sacrifice of Christ is the fullest revelation of divine grace. The believer experiences God's grace in many varied areas such as salvation, sanctification, service and suffering. Grace or favor is sometimes used in Scripture of relationships between people. God's people are divinely enabled to express genuine grace to others. *See Romans 1:5, 1:7, 3:24, 4:4, 5:16, 5:15, 5:17, 5:20-21, 6:1, 6:14-15, 11:5-6, 12:3, 12:6, 15:15, 16:20.*

10. **Justification, Justify or Justified** –The people in the courtroom are filled with anxiety as the jurors bring back their verdict. Then, the judge makes the pronouncement: "Not guilty!" Everyone lets out a sigh of relief. The pronouncement, "not guilty," is what it means to "justify" someone. In common Greek, outside of the New Testament, "justification" and "justify" were frequently used terms in the court of law to describe the act of acquitting or vindicating someone. The Greek noun for "justification," *dikaiōsis*, is derived from the Greek verb *dikaioō*, meaning "to acquit" or "to declare righteous." It is a legal term used for a favorable verdict in a trial. The word depicts a courtroom setting, with God presiding as the Judge, determining the faithfulness of each person to the Law. In the first section of Romans, Paul makes it clear that no one can withstand God's judgment (Rom. 3:9–20). The Law was not given to "justify" sinners, but to expose their sin. To remedy this deplorable situation, God sent His Son to die for our sins, in our place. When we believe in Jesus, He credits His righteousness to us, and we are declared righteous or "not guilty" before God. In this way, God demonstrates that He is both a righteous Judge and the One who declares us righteous, our Justifier (Rom. 3:26). *See Romans 2:13, 3:4, 3:20, 3:24, 3:28, 3:30, 4:2, 5:1, 5:9, 8:30, 16:24.*

11. **Law** - Among the many definitions of law in the English language, two are prominent: (1) a rule of conduct or action which is prescribed, formally recognized as binding, or enforced by a controlling authority; and (2) a statement of an order or relationship between phenomena that so far as is known is invariable under the given conditions (*Webster's Ninth New Collegiate Dictionary*). The first definition can be applied to the laws of this country; the second to a law such as the law of gravity. In the Bible, the first definition is primary; it speaks of God's law, or *nomos* in Greek, for His people. The best known law is the law of God, as revealed through the Ten Commandments. The law revealed at Mount Sinai was intended to lead Israel closer to God. He used the law as His righteous instrument to teach, in a very specific way, the nature of sin (Rom. 5:20; 7:7–8). God also used the law to show the Israelites how to walk on a path that kept them undefiled by sin and holy to the Lord. But all failed; all are sinners worthy of the just punishment for not having kept the law—and this punishment is death. But Jesus paid the price for the penalties of our sins by His substitutionary death on the cross. In the early chapters of Romans, Paul describes the "law" of God and peoples' failure to keep it. Then, in Romans 7–8 Paul speaks of other laws, which fit the second definition noted

above; that is, they are governing principles of action. The first is called "the law of sin," which Paul says was operating through his flesh causing him to sin. But Paul, as with all believers, needed another law to overcome "the law of sin." This is "the law of the Spirit of life in Christ Jesus," which makes us "free from the law of sin and death" (Rom. 8:2). By following this law, believers can actually fulfill the righteous requirements of God's law or rule (Rom. 8:4). Sin always operates in our flesh to cause us to commit sins; it is an invariable law, like the law of gravity. But there is a stronger law, a stronger principle: "the law of the Spirit of life in Christ Jesus." If we cooperate with His Spirit, He can empower us to overcome sin. *See Romans 2:12-2:18, 2:20, 2:23, 2:25-27, 3:19-3:21, 3:27-3:28, 3:31, 4:7, 4:13-16, 5:13, 5:20, 6:14-15, 6:19, 7:1-7:9, 7:12, 14, 7:16, 7:21-23, 7:25, 8:2-8:4, 8:7, 9:4, 9:31-32, 10:4-5, 10:18, 13:8, 13:10.*

12. **Propitiation** – To gain or regain the favor or good will of, to appease or conciliate, atone or satisfy. Because God is holy and vehemently opposed to evil, He will judge sinful mankind. The wrath of God is His just and holy anger directed at man's sin. When Jesus Christ gave His life on the cross, He took upon Himself all of the sin and unrighteousness of man. His blood sacrifice satisfied the wrath of God. Jesus is the propitiation for our sins. All who confess their sin to God and accept Christ as Savior and Lord are forgiven and receive God's grace rather than His wrath. *See Romans 3:25.*

13. **Reconciliation** –Reconciliation involves a changed relationship from enmity to harmony between two parties. In Scripture, reconciliation may indicate (1) the changed relationship between the sinful, alienated world and God, since salvation is divinely provided for mankind through Christ's redemptive work. (2) The believer's actual changed relationship from enmity to peace with God and (3) a change in relationship between human parties from hostility to harmony. *See Romans 5:10.*

14. **Redemption or Redeem** –Redemption involves a payment to liberate someone or something Christian redemption emphasizes the purchase of a slave from his former master (sin) so that he is free to serve his new master (God) Christ's sacrificial death through His shed blood is the ransom price of man's redemption from sin and for God. *See Romans 3:24 and 8:23.*

15. **Repentance** – To turn from sin and dedicate oneself to God; to feel regret; to change one's mind; to feel sorrow. Repentance must follow confession of sin. When the believer truly regrets and is sorry for his sin, he will turn from that sin, dedicate himself to God and walk in God's grace. *See Romans 2:4.*

16. **Righteousness** –The Hebrew and Greek terms translated "righteousness" or "justice" signify that which is right or that which conforms to the character of God. Because God has graciously made a covenant with His people, His righteousness often takes the form of keeping that covenant with acts of deliverance and salvation and judgment on His enemies. The ultimate expression of God's righteousness is seen in the coming of Christ, who works both salvation and judgment. Righteousness is also demanded of man for fellowship with God. This is obtained first through simple faith in Christ resulting in the righteousness of Christ being accounted to the believer. Then the righteousness of God is

gradually incorporated into the practical life of the believer through the ministry of the indwelling Spirit. *See Romans 1:17, 3:5, 3:21, 3:22, 3:25, 3:26, 4:3, 4:5, 4:6, 4:9, 4:11, 4:13, 4:22, 5:17, 5:21, 6:13, 6:16, 6:18-20, 8:10, 9:28, 9:30-31, 10:3.*

17. **Salvation** –The term salvation refers to deliverance from danger, ruin, destruction or sin and into wholeness and safety. The New Testament presents salvation primarily as spiritual deliverance from sin and death and possession of eternal life. Throughout human history, people are saved only by grace through faith, based on the redemptive work of Christ. True salvation results in personal holiness and good works upon earth and culminates in a glorified life with God in heaven forever. *See Romans 1:16, 10:10, 11:11 and 13:11.*

18. **Sin** –Various terms are used in Scripture to describe sin. The most common term in both the Old and New Testaments means to miss the mark, i.e., the righteous standard of God. That such failure is more than mere weakness is seen in other terms that signify rebellion and willful violation of the holy. The basic nature of sin is revealed in the first human sin (Genesis 3). There its essence has been interpreted primarily as unbelief seen in the rejection of God's word or pride in choosing to be as God. Both of these concepts (unbelief and pride) are central to the essence of all sin, which may thus be defined as the willful choosing to be autonomous rather than living by faith under God. Sin results in alienation and separation from God, who is the only source of true human life. The result is death, which is not only viewed as the natural result of sin, but even more as the judgment of God. *See Romans 1:20, 2:12, 3:7, 3:9, 3:20, 3:23, 3:25, 3:30, 4:7, 4:8, 4:19, 5:8, 5:12, 5:13-14, 5:16, 5:19:21, 6:1-2, 6:6-7, 6:10-11, 6:12-18, 6:20, 6:22-23, 7:5, 7:7-7:9, 7:11, 7:13-14, 7:17, 7:20, 7:23, 7:25, 8:1-3, 8:10, 11:27, 14:23, 15:9, 16:25.*

19. **Transgression** - An act of "going beyond" or violating a duty, command, or law. Thus the term connotes lawlessness, iniquity, fault, ungodliness, unrighteousness, and wrongdoing. *See Romans 5:8 and 7:12.*

20. **Wrath, Wrath of God** - Used to express several emotions, including anger, indignation, vexation, grief, bitterness, and fury. It is the emotional response to perceived wrong and injustice. Both humans and God express wrath. When used of God, wrath refers to His absolute opposition to sin and evil. When used of humans, however, wrath is one of those evils that is to be avoided. *See Romans 1:18, 2:5, 2:8, 3:5, 4:15, 5:9, 9:22, 12:19, 13:4-5.*

ENDNOTES

[i] Albert Barnes, Romans 6:15, Accessed 12/01/2015 http://biblehub.com/commentaries/barnes/ephesians/6.htm

[ii] Donald K. Campbell, "Galatians," in The Bible Knowledge Commentary: An Exposition of the Scriptures, ed. J. F. Walvoord and R. B. Zuck, vol. 2 (Wheaton, IL: Victor Books, 1985), 601.

[iii] Kenneth Boa and William Kruidenier, Romans, vol. 6, Holman New Testament Commentary (Nashville, TN: Broadman & Holman Publishers, 2000), ix.

[iv] Martin Luther, Romans, Accessed 12/03/2015, http://www.ccel.org/l/luther/romans/pref_romans.html

[v] C. I. Scofield, Romans Commentary, Accessed 12/27/2015, http://www.preceptaustin.org/new_page_54.htm

[vi] Wiersbe, Warren W. (2010-01-01). The Wiersbe Bible Study Series: Romans (p. 16). David C. Cook. Kindle Edition.

[vii] The Expository Files, Paul's Passion in His Words, Accessed 12/28/2015, http://www.bible.ca/ef/expository-romans-1-14-17.html

[viii] Ray Stedman, 2 Timothy 4:1-4, Accessed 12/28/2015, http://www.raystedman.org/daily-devotions/timothy/preach-the-word

[ix] Alva J. McClain, Romans: The Gospel of God's Grace (Winona Lake, Indiana: BMH Books 2010), 57.

[x] Holman Bible Commentary, 1 and 2nd Corinthians

[xi] Keep Believing Ministries, The Just Shall Live By Faith, August 23,2014, Accessed 12/29/2015 http://www.keepbelieving.com/sermon/the-just-shall-live-by-faith

[xii] McClain, 62.

[xii] Richard L. Pratt Jr, I & II Corinthians, vol. 7, Holman New Testament Commentary (Nashville, TN: Broadman & Holman Publishers, 2000), 22.

[xiii] Precept Austin, Accessed 12/12/2015, http://www.preceptaustin.org/romans_118-19.htm

[xiv] John Piper, The Wrath of God against Holding down the Truth, http://www.desiringgod.org/messages/the-wrath-of-god-against-holding-down-the-truth (September 13th, 1998) Accessed 12/28/2015.

[xv] Dr. Grant C. Richison, Romans Commentary, Accessed 12;28/2015, http://versebyversecommentary.com/romans/romans-121/

[xvi] Charles Spurgeon, Morning and Evening

[xvii] J. I. Packer, Knowing God

[xviii] Ray Pritchard, Mr. I.M. Okay Meets His Maker, Accessed 12/28/2015, http://www.keepbelieving.com/sermon/mr-im-okay-meets-his-maker/

[xix] Alva McClain, Romans: The Gospel of God's Grace p.101

[xx] Wiersbe, Warren W. (2010-01-01). The Wiersbe Bible Study Series: Romans (pp. 33-34). David C. Cook. Kindle Edition.

[xxi] Barclay, William. The Letter to the Romans. (Westminster Press, 1975), pg. 63

[xxii] Barclay, William. The Letter to the Romans. (Westminster Press, 1975), pg. 71

[xxiii] Got Questions.Org, Why does Christ's righteousness need to be imputed to us? Accessed 12/29/2015, http://www.gotquestions.org/imputed-righteousness.html

[xxiv] J. Patout Burns, Theological Anthropology: Sources of Early Christian Thought (Philadelphia, PA.: Fortress Press, 1981), 101.

[xxv]John A. Witmer, "Romans," in The Bible Knowledge Commentary: An Exposition of the Scriptures, ed. J. F. Walvoord and R. B. Zuck, vol. 2 (Wheaton, IL: Victor Books, 1985), 457.

[xxvi] Ray Stedman, Rejoicing in Suffering, Accessed 12/29/2015, http://www.raystedman.org/new-testament/romans/rejoicing-in-suffering

[xxvii] Wilson, Jared C. (2013-04-30). Romans: A 12-Week Study (Knowing the Bible Book 5) (p. 39). Crossway. Kindle Edition.

[xxviii] Paul Johansson, Free By Divine Decree, Living Free of Guilt and Condemnation, Oasis House Publishers, Grandview, Missouri, 2009, p.66-67.

[xxix] Tom Constable, Tom Constable's Expository Notes on the Bible (Galaxie Software, 2003), Ro 6:2.

[xxx] Ibid, Constable

[xxxi] Wiersbe, Warren W. (2010-01-01). The Wiersbe Bible Study Series: Romans (pp. 54-55). David C. Cook. Kindle Edition.

[xxxii] Wiersbe, Warren W. (2010-01-01). The Wiersbe Bible Study Series: Romans (p. 55). David C. Cook. Kindle Edition.

xxxiii James MacDonald, "I'm Dead to That", January 2015, January 2015, http://www.jamesmacdonald.com/teaching/devotionals/2015-01-23/, Accessed 12/30/2015,

xxxiv Mark Vroegop, How to Be an Instrument of Righteousness? October 2014, Accessed 12/30/2015 http://www.yourchurch.com/sermon/how-to-be-an-instrument-of-righteousness/

xxxv Baker's Evangelical Dictionary of Biblical Theology, *Sanctification*, Accessed 12/30/2015, http://www.biblestudytools.com/dictionary/sanctification/

xxxvi Paul Enns, The Moody Handbook of Theology, (Chicago, IL: Moody Press, 1989), 330.

xxxvii Tom Constable, Tom Constable's Expository Notes on the Bible (Galaxie Software, 2003), Ro 7:22.

xxxviii Wiersbe, Romans (pp. 63-64).

xxxix Warren Wiersbe, The Bible Knowledge Commentary New Testament, Cooks Communications, Colorado Spring, Colorado, 2001, p.536

xl The Wiersbe Bible Study Series: Romans (p. 69). David C. Cook. Kindle Edition.

xli Kenneth Berding, A Key Insight From Romans 7 from a Conversation with J.I Packer, Accessed 12/30/2015, http://www.thegoodbookblog.com/2012/apr/04/a-key-insight-about-romans-7-from-a-conversation-w/

xlii Robert H. Mounce, Romans, vol. 27, The New American Commentary (Nashville: Broadman & Holman Publishers, 1995), 44–45.

xliii David Wilkerson Devotions, November 2008, Accessed 12/30/2015, http://davidwilkersontoday.blogspot.com/2008/11/abba-father.html

xliv Calvary Chapel Boise, Romans 8:18-30, Accessed 12.30/2015 , http://www.ccboise.org/sites/default/files/study-guides/guides/COREStudyGuide_21.pdf

xlv Matthew Henry's Concise Commentary, Romans, Accessed 12/31/2015, http://biblehub.com/romans/8-34.htm

xlvi Tom Constable, Tom Constable's Expository Notes on the Bible (Galaxie Software, 2003), Ac 17:27.

xlvii Alva J. McClain, Romans, page 182

xlviii John MacArthur, How do we understand Romans 9:22, "vessels of wrath prepared for destruction"? Accessed 12/31/2015. http://www.gty.org/resources/questions/QA183/how-do-we-understand-romans-922-vessels-of-wrath-prepared-for-destruction

xlix Alva J. McClain, Romans page 184

l Calvary Chapel Boise, Romans 9, Accessed 01/04/2016, http://www.ccboise.org/sites/default/files/study-guides/guides/COREStudyGuide_27.pdf

li Robert H. Mounce, Romans, vol. 27, The New American Commentary (Nashville: Broadman & Holman Publishers, 1995), 208.

lii Robert H. Mounce, Romans, vol. 27, The New American Commentary (Nashville: Broadman & Holman Publishers, 1995), 208.

liii Bible Tools.Org, Romans 10:1-3, Accessed 12/31/2015 http://www.bibletools.org/index.cfm/fuseaction/Topical.show/RTD/CGG/ID/5725/Zeal-without-Knowledge.htm

liv The Wiersbe Bible Study Series: Romans (p. 99).

lv Tom Hovestol, *Extreme Righteousness: Seeing Ourselves in the Pharisees,* Authentic Media, Colorado Springs, 2008, p.62

lvi Vines Word Pictures in the New Testament, Thomas Nelson Publishers, Nashville TN, 2015, p.500

lvii A.W. Tozer, Knowledge of the Holy, Kindle Edition

lviii University Baptist Church, God's Plan for Israel, Accessed, 1/3/2016. http://universitybaptistchurch.com/?sermons=romans-11

lix Biblical Intensives, Romans, Accessed 1/1/2016 http://www.biblicalintensives.com/folio/folio_docs/Romans%20Teacher%20Manual%202009.pdf

lx Powerlife.org, Transformation, Accessed 1/4/2016, http://www.powerlife.org/Consulting/Transforming%20the%20life%20of%20a%20Christian.html

lxi Jay E. Adams, How to Overcome Evil, Philipsburg, New Jersey, P&R Publishing Company 1977

lxii Biblical Training. Accessed 12.16.2015. https://www.biblicaltraining.org/library/adiaphora

lxiii Alva J. McClain, Romans, p.230

lxiv Scott Theological College, A Study of the Book of Romans, Accessed 1/2/2016, http://www2.ministries-online.org/carlfzt/Romans.pdf

37416595R00079

Made in the USA
San Bernardino, CA
17 August 2016